The Mortgage Maze Explained

The Mortgage Maze Explained

Liam Croke

CURRACH PRESS

First published in 2006 by
CURRACH PRESS
55A Spruce Avenue, Stillorgan Industrial Park, Blackrock, Co. Dublin

www.currach.ie

1 3 5 4 2

Cover by Bluett
Origination by Charles Foster
Printed by ColourBooks Baldoyle Industrial Estate Dublin 13

ISBN: 1-85607-934-1

Contents

For Roseann, Rachel and Emily

I
Getting Started

Why it pays to shop around for your mortgage requirements

Whether you are a first-time buyer, trading up, purchasing a property to let or remortgaging, it is good advice first to do your homework on what each of the different lenders in the marketplace currently have on offer. Then, when you make that big decision – with which lender you are going to place your business – it is an informed one.

Arranging a mortgage to purchase your new property can be a daunting task. Where do you start? And more importantly how do you ensure that the mortgage you choose is the best one for you? Because we are all now leading very busy lives we do not have the time to explore in depth the various offers and products that all the lending agencies have to offer.

My experience is that those who choose to arrange a mortgage themselves do one of two things. They may go to the bank where they do their day-to-day banking for convenience and also because they may know the staff or manager and therefore feel that they stand a better chance of getting the mortgage they need. This is fine if that bank is competitive and giving you good advice on the products they have on offer and about which one may best suit your circumstances. However, you are placing enormous trust in your bank that it has placed your interests to the fore and that the advice is given by qualified knowledgeable staff.

The second thing that people do is telephone each bank and ask what rate they are offering and what the monthly repayment on a particular loan amount would be. So what is a bank going to do, knowing you are probably ringing other lenders? Quote their most competitive rate of course, and can you blame them? The lender may not know anything about your personal circumstances and may be quoting you a rate for a product that would be of absolutely no benefit to you in the long term.

The key to choosing the right lender and product for you is that they are suitable and specific to your individual needs and are best suited to your long-term goals.

With over one hundred mortgage variations available in the marketplace, it is essential that you are informed and receive advice as to the different products available and which ones may be more suitable to your present and future circumstances. Lenders will naturally tell you only about their product offering. Don't get me wrong: researching interest rates is an extremely important thing to do but it is also very important that when you are comparing rates you are comparing like with like. One lender may seem very competitive against another, but are you comparing the same products?

Some people tend to think that after a few telephone calls comparing monthly repayments they have researched the market. They then choose the lender with the lowest monthly repayment. How many people opt for a one-year fixed-rate mortgage just because the repayment is the lowest available? Quite a few, to be honest, but many do so without asking what happens when the fixed rate expires. They are then surprised that their monthly repayment has increased by as much as €100 in month thirteen even though interest rates seem to be decreasing. Arm yourself with as much knowledge as you possibly can before deciding on your chosen lender, and then you won't be surprised.

Choosing the best mortgage for you – what to ask!
The product with the most competitive rate is not necessarily the best mortgage for you. There is quite a number of other factors that should come into consideration when you are making your choice. While the rate may ultimately be the overriding factor that sways your decision, you should at least familiarise yourself with other aspects of your chosen product and lender to ensure you are not blindsided by some unexpected cost or restriction.

Apart from rate, the most important aspects of the mortgage product and lender that are worth examining in closer detail are:

- How much is a lender prepared to advance to you. Ask them how they arrive at this figure.
- What percentage of the purchase price is the lender prepared to advance? This is particularly relevant for investors or people who wish to purchase but earn an income from outside the state. It is also relevant for those looking to purchase under an affordable housing scheme. Do you qualify for a 100% mortgage?
- Does the lender allow for additional room rental if you are a single applicant?
- What is the maximum repayment term the lender will allow you?
- Does the lender have any arrangement or indemnity bond fees?
- Can you split your mortgage and have part variable and part on a fixed rate?
- Are you allowed to make over- or under-repayments?
- Can you make lump-sum lodgements without penalty?
- Does the lender have a facility whereby you can make interest-only repayments for a period or maybe for the term of the mortgage?
- Does the lender have a tracker mortgage? If so, how much above the ECB rate are the margins set? Does the lender offer a current-account mortgage?
- If you are remortgaging, up to what percentage of the current value of your property is the lender prepared to advance and can the lender structure your loan so that any short-term debt that was refinanced is still repaid over a shorter term?
- Will the lender pay your solicitor's fees for switching your current mortgage to its company?
- If you are purchasing a site, what percentage of the site cost is the lender prepared to give you up-front?
- Does the lender accept guarantors if your income does not qualify you for the amount you need?

- Will the lender offer you a preferential rate if you are borrowing a certain percentage against the value or purchase price of the property?
- How often is interest charged to your account?
- Will the lender offer you incentives such as discount or fee-free periods on, for example, home insurance, accident and sickness insurance or payment protection insurance? Will the lender pay your valuation fee?
- What methods of repaying your mortgage are available to you?
- Is it possible to release further funds once you have repaid a certain portion of the capital to fund, for example, home improvements, and if so will the rate be the same as your existing home loan?
- Does the lender offer flexible repayment options like skipping a month, taking a mortgage break or deferring your initial repayment?
- Would redemption penalties apply if, for example, you were going to switch to another lender either by selling your property to buy another or simply by remortgaging?

These are just some of the questions you may ask; others will spring to mind that are of particular relevance and importance to you. The idea is that once you have correlated all this information you can then choose from among lenders who will first and foremost advance the amount of money you require. Then the rest of your selection process can be based upon rate, service, flexibility and a product that best suits your own individual requirements.

How much can I borrow?

When assessing how much they will advance to a potential borrower, the majority of lenders now determine this amount on the basis of an applicant's net monthly disposable income so that total monthly repayments including the proposed new mortgage repayment will not exceed a percentage of your take home pay, typically 35%-40%. (The mortgage will be stress-tested at a rate of about 5.5% to ensure that your salary would be capable of meeting repayments should interest rates increase to that level.)

A lender will consider a number of other factors when deciding if they are prepared to advance funds to you, such as: the permanency and security of your employment; satisfactory bank statements; evidence of savings; good repayment history; and the location and condition of the property you intend to purchase. But what they most want to be satisfied with is your ability to repay the amount borrowed.

Until recently the majority of lenders advanced funds to borrowers based upon a multiple of their income, such as 4.5 times their gross income. For a joint application they calculated it by way of 3.5 times the main income and one time the second or some would even use a multiple of 4.75 times the combined income. This method, while still used by some lenders, has been largely replaced by what is now referred to as the net disposable income or debt-service ratio method of calculation.

This new method of calculation differs from lender to lender as all lenders have different means and criteria for their own calculations. For example, for single applicants, some lenders will advance only an amount that when combined with any other monthly commitments – for example a car loan repayment – does not exceed 35% of net take-home pay. Other lenders will allow up to 40%. The difference, which may be substantial, may mean being able to purchase that particular property you wanted – or not. This debt-service percentage may be higher with some lenders, depending on your level of income and your occupation.

Let me give you an example of this difference: let's assume a monthly net income of €2,390 (which is about what you receive if you have a gross basic salary of €35,000 per annum) and a single applicant with no other monthly outgoings. The maximum a lender will advance, based upon total monthly repayments not exceeding 35% of net income, will amount to approximately €181,500 over a 35-year term, whereas a lender who allows for up to 40% will advance €207,500. A significant difference, you will agree.

There are two other very important factors to consider when looking for the maximum amount you qualify for: the term the lender is prepared to offer you; and secondly whether the lender will allow for any rental income you may receive from renting a room or rooms in your property.

Some lenders will advance moneys to borrowers up to a maximum term that does not exceed their 65th birthday, while others will stretch to the age of 70: that is, if you are 30, the maximum term some lenders will give you is a 35-year mortgage whereas others are prepared to offer you a 40-year term. The longer the term, the higher the amount a borrower will qualify for as the monthly repayments will be over a longer period of time

This additional rental income consideration will really apply only to single applicants who are purchasing a property with two or more bedrooms. This additional 'income' a lender may take into account could again have a significant effect on the amount for which you qualify. Some lenders may limit the offer of additional rental income to those on a minimum salary, for example €35,000 or more; others may not have a minimum. Rental income is not freely available and before lenders are prepared to allow it to an applicant they have to be satisfied that the property is situated in an area with a demand for rooms. A lender also has to be satisfied as to the amount a room or rooms would realise, so they are not allowing for an amount that could never be achieved. With each valuation carried out on a property for and on behalf of a lender, the valuer has to give an opinion as to the likely rental income the property would command if it was to be rented; this figure provides evidence for the lender on the basis of which to make a decision.

So let me give you a revised figure based upon your net monthly income of €2,390. If we allow for some room rental and base the mortgage over a 40-year term, now the amount you could expect to borrow has risen from €207,500 to €242,500.

For joint applications the process is very similar. Lenders will look at both incomes and provided that the repayments on an amount the couple are looking for do not exceed a percentage of their take-home pay, taking into account any other loan commitments, then they will be prepared to advance the amount required, assuming that all other criteria are met. It is worth double-checking with your lender, though, as some lenders still only take into account up to a certain percentage of the second, lower, income.

Lenders will also take into account the following when they arrive at the income figure on which to base their calculations:

- Overtime will be taken into account but is normally limited to a maximum of 10% of your basic salary.
- If you have a shift allowance it will be factored in, provided it is confirmed as a permanent and mandatory feature of your job and is evidenced in your payslips and the previous year's P60.
- For commission-based income lenders may allow up to 50% of your basic salary provided the commission can be shown to have been at a consistent level for the previous two or three years and is a regular feature of your job.
- Lenders will normally allow 10% of your basic salary towards a bonus you are likely to receive. As bonuses can be performance-related on both a personal and company level, lenders will be cautious when taking them into account.

If lenders are to take into account any of this additional income on top of your basic, they will need to be satisfied that the income can be achieved and will look for evidence in your current and previous year's earnings.

Standard lending criteria

Typically each lending institution will have standard lending criteria apart from minimum levels of income that will have to be adhered to before they will entertain a loan application. These vary from lender to lender. The following are samples of the criteria:

- The applicant should be aged 18 or over.
- The applicant should have been in continuous permanent employment for a minimum of six months.
- The property to be purchased or used as security should be located in the Republic of Ireland.
- The minimum valuation on the property should be €150,000 in large populated areas and €100,000 in all other areas.
- The maximum age of the applicant on completion of the loan should be 65 or 70, depending on your lender
- The applicant should not be subject to work or visa permit restrictions.
- The applicant should have a good credit history. (See below.)

- The minimum income for single applicants is €20,000 and
  €30,000 for joint applicants. (This may vary depending on
  the amount you are borrowing.)

The above are just a sample of some of the criteria required by
lenders; they will vary from lender to lender.

A note on good credit history

Lenders will do a credit check on you to make sure you have never,
for example, been declared bankrupt or had any judgements
registered against you for non-repayment of a loan or for unpaid
bills. This search will also show a lender whether current or previous
repayments on loans such as car loans or other personal loans have
been made on time and conducted in a satisfactory manner. A credit
check is very important to a lender as it can build a profile for them
about how you have conducted the repayment of any loans you now
have or have had in the past. It is also a safety net for them as it will
show any loans that you did not declare on your application form.

The lenders submit details of your name, address, date of birth
and occupation to the Irish Credit Bureau, which will respond with
details of your credit record. Most lending agencies and financial
institutions are now registered with the credit bureau.

What repayment options are available to me?

Buying a home is the single biggest financial commitment most
people will make in their lifetime. In most cases a mortgage is a
long-term commitment and selecting the right type of mortgage
repayment is crucial. This is generally the first step in the decision-
making process.

There are two options available for the repayment of moneys
borrowed towards the purchase of your home.

The first method is the traditional annuity or repayment type
mortgage, whereby your monthly repayment is made up of two parts,
one part going towards the repayment of the capital sum borrowed
and the second towards repaying the interest charged on the amount
you borrowed.

For example, should you borrow €150,000 over a 30-year term
at a variable rate of 3.50% your monthly repayment would amount

to €673.50 per month (excluding insurances and tax relief). Initially, this repayment is made up of €437.50 going towards the interest repayment portion of the loan and €236.00 towards reducing the capital outstanding. In the early years of your mortgage most of your monthly payment will go towards repaying the interest that is charged to your account and not until approximately the eleventh year will more than 50% of your monthly repayment go towards reducing the amount you borrowed.

The obvious advantage of this method of repayment is that you are guaranteed that at the end of the mortgage term your loan will have been reduced to zero with no further repayments needing to be made. This is, of course, assuming you stay in the same property for the term of your mortgage. Many of us will move two, three even four times during our lifetime and it is reassuring to know that if we do move, whether it be after a year, five years or ten years, each time we will have reduced the amount we originally borrowed under this method of repayment and increased the amount we take with us for our next purchase.

Above all, though, the interest and capital type of repayment gives us peace of mind, knowing that we are reducing the amount we owe each month and that the amount we borrowed is guaranteed to be repaid in full over the term we choose.

The second method of repayment is an interest-only method, whereby the monthly repayment we make to our lender comprises interest only, with no part of the repayment going towards reducing the amount borrowed.

For example, let's look again at borrowing an amount of €150,000 over a 30-year period at a rate of 3.50% variable as we did with the interest and capital-type repayment, but this time on an interest-only basis. In this case the total monthly repayment (excluding insurances and mortgage interest relief) to your lender will amount to €437.50 per month or just €101 per week. The €150,000 you borrowed will stay at the same level as you are not making any inroads into the capital.

The obvious and major advantage of this choice of repayment is cashflow. In the examples shown you are saving €236 each month by opting for the interest-only route. There may be many reasons for opting for this route but there are, I believe, two very important factors to bear in mind.

The first is that that you are not reducing the amount you initially borrowed. Consideration has to be given as to how you will eventually repay the amount you borrowed. It may come from the sale of the property, an expected inheritance or a lump-sum benefit you are entitled to under a pension plan. You may not know at the time you take out this mortgage how you are going to repay it but you must be aware that it does eventually have to be repaid.

So how does a lender have a comfort in knowing you are going to repay the amount they gave you? Well the answer is that some of them do not need to have a comfort because they will just not advance funds by this method of repayment unless the amount sanctioned is, for example, less than 70% of the value or purchase price of the property. However, others will lend greater amounts – even up to 92% of the purchase price – and do recognise that for first-time buyers in particular that the first few months of purchasing a property can be stressful: funds are at a minimum; you are getting used to the fact that maybe a large portion of your income is now going towards this new loan; you need funds to buy furniture and so on; and they will help by offering you this option of repayment. They will offer you the interest-only method for a minimum of three months and up to a maximum of three years so they have a comfort knowing that at the end of the chosen interest-only term the mortgage is then converted into the interest and capital method of repayment (very important to bear this in mind).

One of the mortgage lenders in Ireland is now offering a facility whereby they will advance funds to first-time buyers, people remortgaging or trading up and investors on an interest-only basis for the term of the mortgage without having to get evidence from the borrowers as to how they will eventually repay the amount advanced by them! This is a major new development in mortgage lending here. Part of the reasoning behind this new offering is that statistically the average mortgage term in Ireland is about five years and reducing all the time and the second reason is that Irish houses generally double in value every ten years.

The second factor people should bear in mind is that this method of repayment is available to you if you so wish. No two borrowers are the same: each will have different requirements and needs and advisers should not make up people's minds for them but instead should listen to what they want and advise them of the options available that are most suited to their particular circumstances and best interests. A couple recently brought to my attention that they were advised that they could not repay their mortgage in an interest-only way, a method that would have particularly suited them in their present circumstances and one that could have been made available to them and assisted them a great deal.

Factors that will influence your choice of repayment options

Whether you can afford the proposed mortgage. If your disposable income position is tight, then you may want the lowest gross outlay on your mortgage repayments in the short run, so an interest-only option may suit you so you can put the savings in repayments to better use, buy furniture, repay that gift from your parents etc. After a period of years when your income has increased and maybe you have earned additional income from renting a room in your property, you could then revert to an interest and capital type repayment. It is also worth noting that extending the term of your mortgage from the outset to say 35, or even 40 years will obviously keep your repayments at an absolute minimum and also allow for a comfort should interest rates increase and repayments go up.

Your tax position, particularly for investors. Deferring capital repayments only makes sense, from a financial point of view, if a higher after-tax and expense return can be earned on the funds put aside to repay the mortgage, e.g. pension premiums, compared with the net cost of borrowing, i.e. the interest less any tax reliefs. Therefore, your tax position in relation to the property and the mortgage is of crucial importance.

In general, if full tax relief can be obtained on the mortgage interest paid i.e. for commercial or investment in residential property, deferring capital repayments and going down an interest-only route or pension-backed mortgage may make sense.

Your attitude to risk. This will very much depend on whether you are purchasing a property to reside in yourself or whether you are buying for investment purposes. If it is a property for investment and you are a risk taker, you may opt for an interest-only type repayment method with a view to the property appreciating substantially in value and making a profit on this increase. If the property is a family home, then whether you are a risk taker or not, I would strongly recommend that you make capital repayments if you can, ensuring that the amount borrowed is repaid at the end of the mortgage term.

There are many circumstances to consider and each borrower has to take these on board when making their choice.

Flexible repayment options available

Many lenders have now recognised that a range of flexible repayment options may better suit the individual needs of some of its customers than the two basic types of repayment, interest and capital or interest-only.

This is welcome news particularly to first-time buyers as competition between lenders ensure that the products they offer are reviewed on a regular basis, so that they remain unique and attractive to every potential borrower.

There are some lenders who are now actively marketing a product such as a deferred start option which is specifically targeted at the first-time buyer. The idea behind this is that your monthly mortgage repayments are deferred for a number of months, typically between three and six months, after your loan cheque has issued. The obvious advantage to this type of initial repayment option is that the borrower will benefit from not having any mortgage repayments at a time when cashflow is extremely tight. They may set aside the monthly repayment they would normally have had to make so they can buy furniture for their new property, repay some of that gift they got from their parents etc. The downside to this choice is that the interest portion of the missed monthly repayment is capitalised so your monthly repayment will increase (this will depend on how many months you elect to miss) to ensure your loan is repaid in full over the remaining term.

An interest-only method of repayment as outlined on pages 19-21 is becoming a popular choice for first-time buyers.

The repayment options outlined above are normally targeted

at first-time buyers. There is another product available from some lenders which existing customers can avail of, often referred to as a skipped month option. With this facility customers can opt to skip payments for one or two months during the year. This type of repayment option is of particular use to people who would like to increase their cashflow at times of the year that are normally 'cash-draining' such as summer holidays or Christmas. What happens with the repayments that are skipped is that they are spread out over the remaining months of the year so the term of the loan does not change. The only negative feature of this product is the increased repayments during the remaining months.

There are other options available to existing borrowers such as having a 'mortgage break'. This option is available to clients who have a good track record with their current lender but want to suspend their monthly repayments for a period of time, due to maybe unforeseen circumstances in their lives such as having a child or wanting to travel or have a career break. At the end of the mortgage break the deferred repayments are added back on to the loan so your repayments increase, ensuring that your loan is repaid within the agreed term.

Part fixed and part variable

Another option available to borrowers is splitting your product and rate so that you can have part of your loan on a fixed rate and part at a variable or tracker rate. Therefore should rates increase at least part of your repayment is protected and should rates decrease at least part of your repayment will benefit. Many borrowers are unaware that they can in fact split their loan in two, and this can have an effect on which option they choose.

Choosing your lender

You can now arrange your mortgage from a variety of different sources. Some of the reasons for your choice of lender should be:

- The amount they are willing to lend to you
- How competitive they are
- Customer service
- Flexibility, e.g. overpayments, underpayments, interest-only facilities, 100% mortgages, extend term, mortgage breaks
- Fees, if any
- Reputation – do you know anyone who may have used the particular lender or broker before and how was their experience with them?

The following institutions all offer or arrange mortgages:

Banks
The traditional high-street banks have years of lending experience and have a major presence in most towns and cities in Ireland. In recent years they have become increasingly competitive in the market in response to new entrants in the Irish lending market and the increased competitiveness of the traditional building society. This has led to them to become more innovative and more focused on targeting new and existing mortgage business and the rates and products now offered are a testament to this.

The other advantage of dealing with banks is being able to visit them when you wish, so if you have a problem or need to discuss a particular aspect of your mortgage a face-to-face meeting with them is easily arranged.

There are of course other banks who currently do not have a traditional day-to-day banking presence in the high street here but are very active in the mortgage market. You can conduct your business with them yourself over the phone, through a mortgage broker or indeed via the internet.

Building societies
In the past building societies were seen as the mortgage experts. It was their main business, along with savings accounts. Their product offering was very narrow – mortgages or savings products – but with changes in legislation that allowed them to offer a wider selection of products such as credit cards, car loans and life assurance products, they have become more like banks, albeit in a limited way.

Their primary focus remains to this day mortgage lending whether to owner-occupiers, investors, people trading up or seeking finance to purchase a commercial property. Because of their mutuality their rates are very competitive.

Specialist lending institutions

There are now some mortgage providers who will arrange finance for those who cannot, for whatever reason, obtain a conventional mortgage.

Those who have or had arrears on previous mortgages or other loans in the past and have been refused by other mainstream lenders because of this will fall into this category.

These lenders may not be names you would recognise or have heard of as they mainly operate via mortgage intermediaries.

Insurance companies

Some insurance companies are now offering mortgages to their customer base. Traditionally seen as pension providers and life assurance specialists, they have recognised an opportunity to offer mortgages to their new and existing customers.

They can arrange your mortgage, your home and contents insurance and your mortgage protection requirements all under the same roof and this is one of the reasons they are now offering this additional mortgage service.

They are effectively acting as mortgage intermediaries but may be tied to one particular lending institution. However, the mortgage will be branded and advertised under the insurance company's name.

Mortgage brokers

With the diversity of lending institutions in the mortgage business and the growing number of products available – more than a hundred at the time of writing – the purpose of a mortgage broker is to source and arrange the most suitable product available that will best match their client's expectations and needs. The broker's intention is to take the hassle away from the borrower and make a recommendation that is based on an independent assessment of the suitability of a particular mortgage product. This recommendation will focus on the specific needs of the borrower, ensuring that the bank and product chosen are right for them.

A good broker will go that extra distance to ensure you are well advised of what is and is not available to you and to secure the best possible deal on your behalf.

Choosing a broker who can deal with a number of institutions has obvious attraction. They have an intimate knowledge of each of their bank's lending guidelines, their rates and their service, and they obviously have a number of institutions to choose from should an applicant qualify for the loan amount requested.

Another benefit of choosing a broker who is authorised to deal with numerous lending agencies is that banks vary in how they determine the amount they will advance, for example, to single or joint applicants. This can result in significant differences between banks, so the more banks there are to choose from the better your chance of securing your mortgage.

The broker will liaise with your solicitor, the bank, the builder and of course you, so as to ensure that when a closing date is set and agreed with the vendor/builder the funds will be with your solicitor on this very important date for you. He or she will also deal with any hiccups that may have arisen in the interim.

Some brokers may be tied to certain lenders so you should always ask your broker who they are authorised to deal with, whether they are going to charge you any fees for arranging the mortgage for you and what their qualifications are. You will want to deal with a qualified, knowledgeable individual who is an expert in the area you are seeking advice in, irrespective of whether you arrange your mortgage yourself or through a third party. So, can they explain, for example, what your tax relief will be, if stamp duty is applicable to you and if so how much it will be, What documents are required, and so on.

There are some lenders who do not have a high street presence and will use their appointed mortgage brokers as their sale channel.

The number of mortgage brokers has grown as has their importance and they now account for over 50% of the mortgage market in Ireland.

2
Choosing Your Mortgage Product

Variable-rate mortgages

Variable-rate mortgages have been available for many years. With this type of repayment method your monthly instalment can go up or down during the course of your loan. It can remain unchanged for a considerable period of time and at other times change from month to month.

In general variable-rate mortgages should be lower than fixed rates because the customer will pay an increased rate for the certainty of having a fixed rate. However, this may not always be the case particularly when the expected tendency of market rates is to come down.

Variable rates may suit certain types of customers: those, for example, who feel that rates will come down and may opt for a variable rate in anticipation of this and also those who can afford the increase in repayments should their interest rate increase.

They may also prefer a variable rate as it does not tie them to one particular lender for any period of time and their mortgage can be redeemed in full at any time without penalty. Indeed you can make partial redemptions off your mortgage at any time if you are in a variable rate. This may influence a customer's decision when deciding between fixed or variable as they might know, for example, that they are going to inherit a sum of money which will be used to reduce their mortgage. They might otherwise want to use some or part of their maturing SSIA account to reduce their mortgage, something that can be done without incurring penalties only with a variable rate mortgage.

Of course the other more obvious advantage is that when rates do decrease you would have less to pay each month.

The big disadvantage of a variable-rate mortgage is that you cannot predict with certainty the monthly cost of your mortgage, which can cause problems to those on tight budgets especially in a period when rates do increase.

It is very important to know and bear in mind the effect an increase would have on your monthly repayment should rates increase for example by 0.5% or 1%. Every loan offer letter will now show you by how much your monthly repayment would increase by should rates rise by 1%.

Did you know?

- Variable-rate mortgages are not ideally suited to those on a budget.
- You can redeem your loan in full or make partial large lodgements against the amount outstanding without incurring any penalties.
- May be worthwhile if you think rates will fall as you will benefit from a reduction in your monthly repayment.
- Rates may be higher than some fixed-rate offerings.

Discount variable-rate mortgages

Many lenders offer an initial discount from their current standard variable rate for a certain period of time. The rate will revert to their standard variable rate once the discounted period is up.

For example a 0.76% discount from a lender's current variable rate of 3.70% means your initial repayments would be based upon a rate of 2.94% for the period of the discount, provided the standard variable rate remained at 3.70%. This discount from the standard rate will always remain at this 0.76% level but if interest rates were to increase and your lender decides to increase their rate your repayment will also increase.

The opposite will also happen if rates were to fall – your monthly repayments would fall too. So there is an element of gambling involved with this type of product and it is up to you to judge how comfortable you are with this. In a period of low rates a discounted variable rate can have the effect of making a large mortgage amount look affordable but please be very much aware what your repayments will increase by when the discounted period elapses.

Discount offerings vary in length from six months to two years.

I feel the biggest disadvantage with a discounted mortgage is that at the end of the discounted period your repayments will increase to your lender's standard variable rate, and how competitive is this? I hope this was a question asked by you or, if not, the answer told to you when deciding on the suitability of the product to you. If you are enjoying a substantial discount at a great rate it may mean a hefty rise in repayments and an uncompetitive mortgage rate at the end of the discount period – remember your mortgage may be for a 30- or 35-year period, not for six or twelve months.

The advantage of a discounted rate is that your monthly repayments are based upon an initial low rate which can provide much needed extra cash for other expenses you incurred, particularly buying furniture or decorating your new home. Discounted mortgages are best suited to those who wish to avail of an initial low repayment rate but can afford any increased repayments following the end of the discounted period.

Did you know?

- This type of product is discounted from a lender's current standard variable rate for an initial period.
- Discounted periods range from six to 24 months.
- Not ideally suited to those on a budget.
- Good for those who want their repayments as low as possible to start out with and can afford the increase in repayments following an end to the discounted period.

Fixed-rate mortgages

Fixed-rate mortgages are the straightforward, reliable product that everyone understands. They are good for first-time buyers and anyone who is on a budget and needs the stability of a set monthly repayment.

The concept is this: no matter what happens to base rates, your monthly repayment will remain the same for the duration of the fixed period chosen.

They are rarely the cheapest mortgages on the market (depending on the fixed period chosen) but nonetheless there is a range of different fixed-rate products to choose from that are now available from most lenders that are very competitive and offer stability at an affordable cost. Current low interest rates have also narrowed the gap between fixed and variable rates with some fixed-rate offerings lower than standard variable rates.

With a variable-rate mortgage, your payments will go up or down according to the European Central Bank's base rate. If interest rates go up, fixed-rate customers will know for certainty that their repayments will remain unchanged following the increase. On the flip side however, it will also mean that if the rates decrease and stay low for a period of time, your repayments will remain as high as they ever were for as long as the fixed period lasts. Many people will remember back to the early 1990s when rates increased to very high levels in a very short space of time and due to uncertainty as to whether rates would continue to increase many people had no option but to fix their rate for peace of mind. Many people chose fixed terms in excess of five years at rates from 10%. Unfortunately, it turned out to be an unwise thing to do as rates did return to normal – averaging at about 5.5%. At that time many people were paying way over the odds and faced being penalised heavily for breaking the fixed-rate agreement either by switching lender or by moving house. At times, the penalty was so high it meant neither was an option.

Even if interest rates do remain level, you are still probably going to pay slightly over the odds because fixed rates tend to be offered at a higher initial rate than variable ones, but this is considered a bearable premium for the peace of mind that a fixed rate gives you.

The rate offered for fixed rates will depend on the length of time you decide to fix for. So the shorter the fixed-rate term the lower the rate and the longer you decide to fix for the higher the rate is and subsequently the higher your monthly repayments will be. You can fix from periods of one to ten years and rates vary from as little as 2.94% to 4.60% depending on the fixed term chosen.

It is very important for you not to fix for longer than you think you will be comfortable with, as one of the main disadvantages of fixed rates is that if you wanted either to remortgage or move to another property before the fixed rate expires, you might have to pay a sizeable early redemption penalty for doing so, as stated earlier. So when choosing a fixed-rate term make sure you can afford the monthly repayments and secondly make sure that you will be in your new house, to the best of your knowledge at the time of deciding, for at least the same period as the fixed rate so you can avoid early redemption penalties.

With rates being so low, the temptation to fix for a long time is strong and people who have large financial commitments and look likely to remain on a tight budget for several years could benefit from fixing for a longer period of time so as to avoid having to meet larger monthly repayments should rates increase

It makes sense to choose a fixed rate if you think rates are likely to increase. Rates are at record lows, and whilst fixed-rate mortgages are becoming a very popular choice particularly with first-time buyers and because of the savings that may be made, no one can be absolutely certain which way rates will go.

What happens after your fixed rate expires? Your lender will normally write to you about a month before your fixed-rate period expires and outline the options available to you. So you will be given an option to choose a fixed rate for another year, two, three or ten, or maybe revert to a variable-type repayment. When choosing your lender, always ask whether the rate offered to you when you were a new customer will be the same when the fixed-rate period is up for renewal. Some lenders may distinguish between new and existing business and increase the rate for existing customers. The difference can be substantial.

Did you know?
- Ideal for first-time buyers or those on a budget.
- High redemption penalties can apply should you break your fixed-rate agreement.
- Worth considering if you think rates are on the increase.
- Your monthly repayment will remain the same for the duration of the fixed rate chosen.

Tracker mortgages
Lenders have the right to change their standard variable rate regardless of changes to the European Central Bank base rate although the majority broadly follow it. Tracker mortgages bypass this by mirroring exactly any changes to the ECB base rate.

Interest rates on a tracker mortgage are charged at a set

percentage above the ECB base rate and will vary depending on (a) the amount you are borrowing against the value of the property you are offering as security, so typically the lower the risk to the bank the better the rate they are likely to offer and (b) the rate may also depend on the amount you are borrowing and may decrease above a certain threshold. The margin set above the ECB base rate will remain constant for the duration of the mortgage or until you switch product or lender.

Tracker mortgages offer some security as the rate is guaranteed never to exceed the base rate by more than a fixed margin. Payments will fluctuate over time as the ECB's base rate increases or decreases so they may not be suited to those on a strict budget.

With a tracker mortgage, you will benefit instantly from any drop in interest rates, which means you will know immediately what your rate will be as soon as the European Central Bank announces it. If your mortgage is on a standard variable rate with your lender, you may have to wait and see what it does and even then you may not significantly benefit from any cuts passed on by the ECB.

There was some controversy regarding this a couple of years back when the ECB reduced rates by approximately 0.5% but many of the banks reduced their rates only by 0.25% and did not pass on the full rate cut. It took considerable pressure from lobby groups and indeed the government for lenders to pass on the full rate reduction. I believe bad press was a factor also as when one bank announced that they had now passed on the full reduction everybody knew which bank hadn't done so.

With a tracker mortgage, if rates do fluctuate this will have an effect on your monthly repayment, a rise will increase your repayment and a decrease obviously reduces your monthly repayment. So it makes budgeting more difficult and if you cannot afford for rates to increase by more than a certain percentage you may not want to take the risk with this type of product or indeed any type of variable-rate product.

As stated, the rate applicable to a tracker mortgage is linked to ECB base rate, but by how much will it exceed this rate? Well, that depends on the amount you wish to borrow and the value of your home (loan to value). The rate will be determined by these factors and the lower the loan to value the lower the percentage above the ECB base rate will be. For example, if you are borrowing less than 60% of the value of your property, the margin charged may, for example, be 0.95%, so your mortgage rate would be 3.20%, i.e. ECB base rate currently at 2.25% plus margin of 0.95%. If the loan is above 85% of the value of the property, the margin charged could be between 1.15% and 1.55% depending on the lender. The difference can be significant so it pays to shop around.

The advantage of a tracker mortgage is that if you have a loan with a low loan-to-value ratio, your mortgage rate could be as low as 3.00% compared to the lowest standard variable rate in the market which is 3.50% at the moment. There is a significant difference in repayments here. Also, you have a guarantee that your mortgage rate will always be linked to the ECB base rate and that your rate will always be within a certain margin of it.

The method of repayment of a tracker mortgage is exactly the same as all other mortgages, in that you can make interest and capital type repayments or indeed interest-only type repayments. Additionally, you have the facility to make overpayments on a monthly basis or lump sum repayments to the amount outstanding.

Did you know?

- This type of product directly follows the changes in the base rate of the European Central Bank.
- The margin set above the base rate will depend on the amount you are borrowing and your loan-to-value i.e. the amount of your loan as a percentage of the value of your property.
- You will benefit from decreases in your repayments with rate reductions but you are also exposed to the risk of your monthly repayment increasing should rates rise, so this product is not suited to those who are working on a budget.
- You know what the margin charged above the base rate is and will always know this so it is in some ways a fairer system than the way standard variable rates are determined.

Current-account and offset mortgages

Both types of mortgage accounts are a relatively innovative approach to personal finances. The basic idea behind the offset and current-account mortgage involves pooling some or all of your financial assets and obligations into one place.

With an offset mortgage account, all your finances are interlinked so your mortgage, current account and any other savings account you have are with the same lender. Basically the accounts you hold in a credit manner, i.e. savings and current account, are offset against those that are in a debit situation, i.e. mortgage account.

So for example, let's assume you have a mortgage where the balance outstanding is €150,000 and the interest rate charged to this account is 3.5%.

Alongside this, your financial assets are placed into a combination of your current account where your salary is lodged into and a savings account, both with the same bank you have your mortgage with. Let us assume that you have €9,000 held in the savings account and an average daily balance in your current account of €1,000.

With an offset mortgage, the lender will normally not pay interest on your €9,000 savings in the traditional way. Instead, rather than charge 3.5% on your €150,000 mortgage, they charge interest on the €150,000 minus the €9,000 in savings and the €1,000 in your current account, thus charging interest in total on your mortgage account on €140,000 rather than €150,000.

This means that your €9,000 would, in essence, be accruing interest at 3.5%. If this 3.5% was paid to you normally, tax would be owed on the interest earned. If the lender deducts this from your mortgage interest rather than paying it to you, it means there will be no tax to pay, resulting in an effective net interest of 3.5%. To get this sort of return on a normal investment, you would usually have to earn around 5% gross (before tax), although this depends on your annual income.

The effect of using this type of mortgage account in the correct manner could result in saving you money in interest charges and the earler repayment of your mortgage than you previously anticipated.

Current account mortgages work in much the same way. With this type of account you have a mortgage and current account (where your salary is lodged) and again the amount of money in your operating current account is helping to reduce what you owe on your mortgage account.

Interest is calculated on a daily basis on your mortgage account so the more you have in your current account the less interest is being charged to your mortgage account each day.

As it is your current, and probably your main day-to-day operating account the balance will naturally reduce during the course of the month. However even a relatively small amount left in your account at the end of each month could lead to a substantial saving in total interest repayments made by you, resulting in repaying your mortgage early.

With this type of account your monthly repayment can be based upon either the difference between your mortgage account balance and what is in your current account at the end of each month – your repayment may differ each month under this option – or a monthly repayment planned from the outset that will repay the amount borrowed over the term of the mortgage (the amount left over each month in the current account will help reduce the term of your mortgage).

You can also make additional lump-sum payments to your mortgage without penalty if you wish.

Both types of accounts are very welcome to the mortgage market here and there has been a rapid increase in the number of people opting for this type of facility. With SSIA accounts maturing this year, people will have been used to setting aside a certain amount of money each month but with no replacement for the SSIAs and therefore no government bonus being added to your savings you would not go far wrong in considering this type of repayment method for your present mortgage and continuing making the payment you previously were saving each month not into a savings account but into your mortgage account. Let me give you an example of this: if you borrowed €200,000 over a 20-year period and left €254 in your current account each month, you would repay your mortgage five years sooner, saving yourself over €20,000 in interest.

There are currently two lenders in the market who are offering this types of mortgage accounts, but I expect other lenders to follow suit.

Did you know?
- Suitable for people who are good at controlling and monitoring their finances on a monthly basis.
- You can still make over- and under- repayments to your mortgage account.
- Ideal for those who have a mortgage and also have medium to large savings

accounts that are earning very little deposit interest.

- You can repay your mortgage in a much shorter period of time if you operate the account in a proper manner, but you have to be dedicated and committed to this course of action.

100% mortgages

The costs associated with purchasing a property will typically include legal fees, valuation fees and possibly a structural survey. Stamp duty may apply to your purchase and, as lenders normally limit the amount they advance to borrowers to a maximum of 92% of the purchase price of the property, an additional cost and the single biggest contribution a purchaser has to make towards the property is contributing 8% of the purchase price themselves.

This 8% was a big ask, especially for first-time buyers who may have had to save, for example, €24,000 if the purchase price of the property was €300,000, before paying legal fees or purchasing furniture for their new property.

The frustrating thing, especially for first-time buyers, was that between the time they started saving and the time they had saved the required amount, prices of property might have increased and increased substantially, so they were in a Catch-22 situation: do they wait and save or do they try and get the money from somewhere such as a credit union or a gift from a parent, and purchase now.

It was also very frustrating for many first-time buyers because they could easily afford the monthly repayments on the amount they needed to borrow and at times were paying more per month for their rented accommodation than what their own repayment would be on a mortgage. However, many just could not purchase because they were unable to fund the 8% towards the purchase price.

So July 2005 brought great news to those first-time buyers who were caught in the rental trap when some lenders began offering a 100% mortgage facility to those who met with their requirements.

If you are a first-time buyer you can now effectively buy a property without having to contribute anything towards the purchase apart from your legal and valuation fees. Typically you will have to pay 10% on signing of contracts which the bank may not fund (this depends on the lender) but this can be reclaimed by you when your loan cheque for the full 100% issues.

The majority of lenders who operate a 100% mortgage facility will now facilitate up to 10% of the purchase price to the borrower on signing contracts. This is done by way of either a part drawdown of the loan amount or by a personal loan. The cheque will be furnished to the borrower's solicitor and it will be conditioned in the offer letter that this 'loan' is cleared from the full loan cheque when issued.

This 100% facility is not totally new to the Irish market. Some lenders have advanced 100% mortgages in the past to those they felt were a lower risk. These borrowers would normally have to be of a certain profession, such as accountants, dentists, doctors, lawyers, vets or pharmacists.

As lenders are exposing themselves to a higher risk than they have done in the past, they have naturally set down some guidelines which have to be strictly adhered to. They include the following:

- You have to be in continuous permanent employment for at least three years (some lenders may consider one year of continuous employment).
- 100% facility is available only to first-time buyers purchasing a property to live in as their principal private residence.
- No interest-only facilities will be made available.
- No guarantors will be involved in the loan agreement.
- Not available to those purchasing a one-bed apartment.
- Not available for site purchase.
- The term of the loan may be limited to 30 years (depends on lender).
- Repayment ability may be stress-tested at a rate of about 5.70% with total loan commitments including your new loan repayment not exceeding between 35 and 40% of your take-home pay.
- You have to submit six months' current accounts to your lender and they have to be to the satisfaction of your lender. A referral fee or an unpaid direct debit appearing on them may result in the lender not offering you a 100% facility
- Additional income for renting a room may be allowed, depending on the lender.

- If it is a joint application, at least one of the borrowers has to be a first-time buyer.
- Some lenders may impose minimum income requirements, such as €35,000 for single applicants and €65,000 for joint applications.

These are just some of the qualifying criteria and they may vary from lender to lender.

So once the above criteria are to a lender's satisfaction and you can clearly demonstrate that you have the capacity to repay the amount sought, then you could well be on your way to becoming a home owner.

There are some considerations that you should be aware of when deciding if the 100% facility is the best route for you to take. You may be vulnerable to price fluctuations in the housing market depending on where your property is situated and if prices were to drop, selling your property may not generate sufficient money for you to repay the mortgage in full and you could find yourself in a negative equity situation. i.e. your house is worth less than the money borrowed on it.

Of course if you never decide to sell your property, whether your house is in a negative equity situation or worth a whole lot more than your mortgage will not matter as you are still paying off the mortgage secured on it.

It is far more important for first-time buyers to be more comfortable with their monthly repayments by taking on a 100% facility than to be worrying about falling house prices. So 100% mortgages should not be taken on by those who are using the facility to purchase a property with a view to living in it for a short time.

The big advantage of a 100% mortgage is that it will allow first-time buyers to get on to the property ladder without having to have, for example, savings in excess of €24,000 or be burdened with that gift they received from their parents and have to worry about repaying them. Whatever savings they have can now be used to meet other house-buying costs.

Did you know?

- Ideal for first-time buyers with little savings who want to enter the property market.
- Lending criteria as set out by each lender will have to be met in full.
- You are vulnerable to possible fluctuations in house prices.
- Rates may differ from if you are borrowing 92% or less of the purchase price of a property.

Adverse credit mortgages

Adverse credit mortgages are the rough-and-ready name for mortgages that are just as likely to be found under a number of other guises, including impaired or bad credit mortgages. Between them, they are now beginning to account for a large section of the mortgage market. It used to be the case that if you didn't have a perfect credit record you couldn't get a mortgage from a lender. But now, the lending market has become so diverse that there are products to fit every credit profile.

People may have been refused credit due to:

- Mortgage arrears
- No proof of income
- Poor credit rating
- Contract work
- Judgements registered against them

Today there are products that are aimed specifically at those people with some form of impaired credit history. These mortgages do not differ vastly from other mainstream mortgages – you can usually find discounted, fixed, or even tracker rates available with adverse credit mortgages.

However, there are certain key differences between them and standard mortgages.

Impaired credit mortgages have historically charged rates of interest that are significantly higher than normal mainstream mortgages, often charging a premium of one, two or even three percent more than mainstream conforming mortgages.

The interest rates will depend on the particular product: for instance whether it is fixed or variable; your degree of bad credit;

if a judgement was registered against you how much it was for; and finally, if you have or have had a mortgage or any other loan, how many months' arrears you have. All these factors will determine the interest rate offered and the difference can be significant. It is impossible to find deals and offers that are as competitive as those offered to mainstream borrowers.

The approach to underwriting on the part of the lender is also different: most lenders that service this sector of the market adopt a case-by-case approach. A non-conforming lender is likely to be rather more conservative in terms of the amount that they are willing to advance. As well as being less willing to loan large sums of money, adverse credit lenders are usually more demanding in terms of the size of the deposit you are required to contribute to the asking price of your chosen property if you are a first-time buyer or trading up. Many impaired credit lenders are willing to advance no more than 90% of the property value depending on your credit history, reducing to 75% to those with particularly bad credit.

A final feature of many impaired credit mortgages, although one that is not by any stretch unique to them, is the fact that there can be extremely severe early redemption penalties. These can be more onerous than with mainstream mortgages both in the size of the penalty that will apply and in terms of the length of time for which the penalty period lasts.

Did you know?

- An adverse mortgage can help those who have a poor credit history to purchase or remortgage,
- Rates are higher than normal mortgages.
- It may be possible to remortgage after a number of years once an excellent proven track record can be shown.
- You may need a higher initial deposit depending on how bad your credit history is.

3
First-Time Buyers

Rent or buy?

Ireland has become obsessed with house prices. Given the coverage that the subject receives, it is difficult to be blind to the financial benefit that the steady or surging long-term gains of property ownership brings. It is unsurprising then that young professionals are so keen to get started on the property ladder.

However, thanks largely to rising house prices that make home ownership so appealing, many first-time buyers simply can't afford or find it very difficult to get together a deposit of a sufficient size to meet the loan-to-value requirements on most mortgages, or may not qualify for a 100% mortgage based on their current income.

So do you continue to rent or buy? For most it is not a tough decision to make. Of course the majority of us want to own a property we can call our home but purchasing it is not as simple as some would like it to be!

There are many who are currently renting and have become increasingly frustrated as they may be paying more in rent than they would be if they were repaying a mortgage. Each week, I meet single people and couples where this is the case. Well, why do they not buy a house, you may ask, when affordability and repayment capacity are not an issue? These factors may indeed not be the problem but lack of savings is!

Those who are renting and are trying to save for their own property are in a tough situation because along with paying rent, trying to save and also have some sort of a life, in the time it will take to them to accumulate the amount they require, the purchase price of many properties will have substantially increased, along with the amount they will need to borrow.

The saving grace for many of these people caught in the 'rental trap' is the 100% mortgage offering now available from a variety of mortgage providers. This may be the only way possible for them to purchase a property of their own.

Ideally, though, the deposit required would have been saved as this will lower the amount you need to borrow, thereby lowering your monthly repaymentd. You are also carrying some bit of equity with you should you wish to upgrade in the future.

Get on the ladder! Solutions for first-time buyers

It can be difficult to get the amount sanctioned by a lender to buy your first home. With house prices rising faster than salaries, it may not be possible to obtain a loan approval based on a single or joint income alone. In some cases, the following options may be available to you which may assist your application and help to get you the amount you need.

Rent-a-Room scheme

This was introduced in the Finance Act 2001. Under this act if you rent out a room(s) in a property in the state deemed to be your principal private residence and occupied by you you are allowed to receive up to €7,620 in rental income, including the cost associated with the supply of services such as laundry and telephone without having to pay any tax. This is in stark contrast to the situation before this act when any additional income you received from renting out a room in your property was taxable.

Many lenders will include this additional rental income on top of your income earned from employment, which may increase the amount you can qualify for. Some lenders will factor in this rental income provided you are earning in excess of a certain amount each year. Other lenders may limit the amount given as rental income and may set a ceiling per month that they will not go beyond even if you are getting more.

Of course it will vary from lender to lender whether they will include this additional source of income for you or not, so just ask your lender if they will factor it in and if so how much they will allow.

Guarantors

In some cases your parents can act as guarantors for you, allowing you to borrow more than you would otherwise have been allowed. A lender may, however, allow a guarantor only if there is a small shortfall, typically between €15,000 to €30,000 of the amount required.

The other thing to bear in mind is that if you are applying for a 100% facility a lender will not allow for a guarantor when determining repayment capacity.

If you default on your mortgage repayments the guarantor will be liable, so make sure the guarantor is fully aware of what they are undertaking.

Some lenders may accept guarantors only provided their income is above a certain amount so check first with your lender if this is applicable and if so, what this income level is.

Joint applicants

Lenders may consider a second applicant to the mortgage when the applicant is joining in on the mortgage for income purposes only and will not appear on the title deeds of the property. This may save on stamp duty if the second applicant is not a first-time buyer and on capital gains when selling the property but explore this more with your solicitor as there is a grey area at the moment as to whether stamp duty may apply.

This option is normally used if the shortfall is quite big and all the second applicant's income is required. When determining whether the combined income is sufficient a lender will also factor in the second applicant's outgoings – this is important to bear in mind.

Buy in a cheaper location

This is not an easy solution but if you simply cannot afford a home in your ideal location consider purchasing somewhere else that is in your price range. Properties in up-and-coming areas bordering already popular areas that may be undergoing regeneration could be in your price range now and could possibly increase in value in the future.

Liens

This is where a bank may agree to advance funds to you, where you do not qualify under their standard lending criteria, for instance as a result of income shortfall, provided you first place a sum of money on deposit with them to which you will have no access until your loan has reduced to a certain amount.

Liens can also be placed on, for example, a savings account belonging to your parents that is held with the lender who is advancing the mortgage to you.

Buy a property in need of renovation

We are often put off by properties that need quite a bit of work. They obviously cost less but if you are willing to put in the effort and enjoy doing some hard work yourself it can be a very rewarding exercise.

It would be advisable to get a structural survey carried out on the property first to ascertain if the property is at least structurally sound. Get detailed costings of the work needed to renovate the property to the condition you are going to be happy with and finally check if planning permission would be required on the work you intend to carry out.

Buy with a friend

Purchasing a property with a friend may be worth considering if both are unable to borrow in their own name. Combining your income not only increases your borrowing capacity; you can share the costs involved, including legal fees and furnishing the property.

Affordable housing scheme

The reason for the introduction of this scheme was to assist those on lower incomes to purchase their own property. Property prices in many areas in towns and cities across Ireland were just too expensive and unaffordable to many on lower incomes. So some of the properties in developments have been offered for sale to first-time buyers at prices considerably less than the market value.

To check for availability for houses for sale under this scheme you should check first with your local authority.

Mortgages to purchase these types of properties are available from many mainstream lenders. The amount can be up to 97% of the contract price of the property but this can vary from lender to lender.

In order to qualify you must first:

- Register with your local authority on their housing waiting list
- Satisfy the income criteria required to qualify, which for a single income household is a gross income of €36,800 or less. If there are two incomes, the combined total can not be more than €92,000 when the higher income is multiplied by 2.5 and added to the second income.
- Show that you are currently a local authority tenant or tenant purchaser, you wish to purchase a private home and you will return your current property to the local authority

Steps to mortgage success

When it comes to applying for a mortgage, time really is of the essence. If you have found your dream home and you don't have your mortgage in place you could miss out. So whether you are applying in a hurry or in advance, there are things you can do to ensure that your application is a quick and painless procedure.

Whether you are dealing with a mortgage broker or directly with your bank, you can only benefit by making things as clear and straightforward as possible. Some of the points I will outline may seem very basic and obvious, but it is surprisingly easy to overlook the simple things in the midst of the whole mortgage process.

Mortgage checklist

Each lending agency will require a number of documents from you before they will process an application for you. Typically what they will need is:

- **Mortgage application form.** This is a form which will outline your personal, employment and financial details together with the address of the property you are purchasing, loan amount required, solicitor's details etc.
- **Income verification.** A letter from your employer confirming income, permanency of employment, how long you are with the company, your occupation, and whether you are subject to a probationary period. These questions, along with others, can be completed by your employer on a standard form supplied to you by the lender, called a salary certificate
- **Accountant's report form.** This is a form completed by the accountant of a self-employed person confirming, for example, gross earnings for the previous three years, net profit made by the company, the company's net worth, confirmation that tax affairs are up to date etc. This type of form may be sufficient, depending on the lender, although it would not be unusual for a lender to want to see a full set of audited accounts for the previous three years in addition to this form.
- Your last **P60**
- Three recent **payslips**
- Six months **current account statements**
- Twelve months **loan account statements** if you have a current loan outstanding
- Up to date **mortgage statement** if you have a current mortgage
- **Evidence of your contribution** towards the purchase, should you be borrowing 92% or less. So if this is coming from your own savings an account statement showing the funds will suffice. If it is coming by way of a gift from a parent some lenders will require evidence that they have funds in their account along with a gift letter from them confirming the amount they are gifting you.
- **Evidence of your identity.** Your passport or driver's licence will suffice here.
- **Confirmation of your current address.** This is evidenced by way of a utility bill. Check with the lender or broker as to what type of utility bills are acceptable as this will vary from lender to lender.

Step 1 (Application)

Now that you have gathered the above together you are in a position to submit an application to a lender for approval.

Before you do, though, make sure for example that you double-check that the application form is completed correctly. Do not assume that the person reading the form knows you, even if you are an existing customer of the bank. Fill in the information you are asked for and don't leave anything blank, including simple things like phone numbers, dates of birth, employment details, income, existing financial commitments, bank account numbers. If you don't give the correct information or fail to complete the form in full, your application will suffer and will be delayed.

If it is a joint application, sign and date in every single place you are asked to. You will also be asked to sign a section in the application form referring to consent under the Consumer Credit Act 1995, for credit reference and sharing, and consent under the Data Protection Act 1988. These must be signed as a lender will not even look at your proposal unless these sections are signed and dated by you both.

Ensure you enclose: payslips, P60s, current account statements, loan statements, salary certificates, ID, utility bill etc. Check first with the lender whether they require records dating back 12 or 24 months. You will be told when interviewed what will be required and given a mortgage checklist as outlined above. Return all items along with the application as this will help the lender to make a quicker decision on your application; they may not be able to assess your application fully without first having evidence of your current account statements or payslips, for example. It is not impossible that the documents provided by you will be lost by the lender, so for safety's sake, keep photocopies for your own records.

When you submit your application, try and make sure you are returning the forms to the relevant person, that is ideally the person with whom who you originally had the interview. Many lenders now have several different lending sections at one branch so make sure your application is clearly marked for the person you want it to get to and if you do not meet them face to face when submitting your application, telephone them to confirm that they did in fact receive your forms.

After four to five days, follow up on the progress of your

application if your lender has not already contacted you with their decision. You will be anxious to know if your loan has been approved so don't be afraid to call the lender or your mortgage broker to check on the application's current status.

If there are additional items your lender needs from you, find out what they are and why they are needed and return them as soon as you can.

Step 2 (Approval in principle)

OK, you should now have received a decision from a lender as to whether they are prepared to advance you the amount of loan you requested.

Typically this will come in writing from the lender in the form of an 'approval in principle'. This approval in principle is a conditional offer made by a lender to you based on the information you supplied to them with your application form. They will agree in principle to sanction the amount you looked for from them.

This is a very useful thing to have and is your starting point even before you have begun searching for a property. Knowing exactly what you can afford will also help narrow your search as you can now look to purchase a property in a particular price range, confident in the knowledge that your mortgage has been approved.

Step 3 (Approval in principle to full offer)

If you are bidding on a property and are successful or wish to place a deposit on a new/second-hand property you need to start arranging your full letter of loan offer quickly.

Once you have placed a deposit, you will be asked the name and address of the solicitor who is going to act for you in your purchase. The reason for this request is so that contracts can be sent to your solicitor for examination. Your solicitor will look at the conditions of sale and title documents, and explain to you in detail the terms and conditions of the contract. If you are happy to proceed the contracts will need to be signed by you and returned to the vendor's solicitor along with a deposit, which is typically 10% of the purchase price.

Once your bid has been accepted or your deposit placed on your new or second-hand property, your solicitor could be in receipt of contracts within a week or two after the deposit had been placed;

hence the urgency of having your full offer letter at hand. You do not want to enter into a legally binding agreement for the purchase of a property without definite knowledge that your loan has been fully sanctioned, thereby putting your 10% deposit at risk. It is worth noting at this point that until contracts have been signed by both parties either party can withdraw.

You are normally given 14 days to return signed contracts along with your 10% deposit. If contracts are with your solicitor but no formal offer letter from a lender has been received your solicitor may insert a clause in the contract stating 'subject to loan approval'. This allows you to sign the contract with a possible escape clause should you be refused finance. However, it is frequently the case nowadays that the vendor's or developer's solicitor will refuse to accept a contract with this clause inserted.

So how do you get that formal offer letter? If you have an approval in principle (AIP) already in place it will state exactly what the lender will require in order to issue your full offer letter. For example, your AIP may state you have been approved in the amount of €X and in order for a formal offer to issue they will require satisfactory valuation (with photograph) of the property carried out by a valuer appointed by your lender.

There may be other conditions attaching to the AIP: for example documents that you failed to submit originally, such as P60s, up-to-date bank statements, photo ID or address verification. These are items that your lender may need before they issue your offer letter. Some lenders may just go straight to an offer letter with all these conditions inserted in the offer.

So what do you do? You tell the bank or your broker that your offer has been accepted and that you need your offer letter ASAP. They will then tell you what is and is not required and what needs to be done. Let's assume you have submitted everything and a valuation on the property is the only item outstanding. Each lender has a panel of valuers and the valuation report on your property will have to be completed by a firm who are approved by the lender. The cost associated with a valuation fee is typically €127 and each lender will instruct that a report be carried out on the property they are mortgaging.

When the completed valuation report is returned to your lender they are now in a position to furnish you with your formal offer letter. You will receive this within a matter of days. They will also forward a legal pack to your solicitor which includes amongst other things a copy of the loan sanction, copy of the valuation report and solicitor's undertaking. Now your solicitor and you have evidence that you will have sufficient funds for the purchase, subject to adherence to your conditions and your being happy with and accepting the offer.

You can now sign contracts in confidence with great peace of mind.

Step 4 (Loan offer)

When the lender receives the valuation report, before they will issue the offer they will of course need to know what term and product – for instance, fixed or variable, tracker or discounted variable – you wish to appear on your formal loan sanction letter. It is prudent, therefore, to discuss with your lender either prior to or whilst waiting for that valuation to come back which product best suits you and which is the one you are most comfortable with so when that offer does issue it has the correct information recorded as per your instructions.

If a lender goes straight to offer without first needing a valuation on the property it is wise to meet them again to reaffirm what you had discussed with them previously, have any final questions answered and decide on a plan of action.

OK, your loan offer has issued. What is the next step?

Step 5 (Arranging completion)

You need to start making arrangements to close the purchase on the date specified in the contract or on a date agreed between you and the vendor.

If the property is second-hand it may be easier to agree an exact closing date, especially if it is unoccupied. If the property is new and under construction it may be a little bit more difficult.

Typically there will be a number of conditions that you will have to adhere to before a lender will release funds to your solicitor. The standard conditions are:

Mortgage protection policy

A lender will insist that life cover in the amount of the loan and for the term of the mortgage is in force prior to drawdown. The lender will want to see the policy document in its original form or at least a copy of the original policy document

They will further insist that this life policy is 'assigned' to the lender as additional security so you will complete a 'notice of assignment' which is a standard form included in your solicitor's legal pack.

If you elect to repay by an interest-only method the lender will double-check your policy document so as to ensure that the policy is a level term policy (see insurances on page 107)

Home insurance

Each lender will want their interest noted in a suitable home insurance policy which will have the property covered for at least the reinstatement amount recommended in the valuation report carried out on the property.

They will require either evidence of the policy schedule noting their name and address in the policy, the reinstatement value, the borrower's name and address and/or a 'letter of indemnity' from the insurance provider. The policy must be fully comprehensive and index linked.

If the property is an apartment there will be a block insurance policy in place covering yours and other owned apartments. The lender will require evidence that the policy schedule of the unit purchased notes the borrower's interest along with that of the lender.

Direct debit mandate

Before your lender issues your loan cheque they will require that you complete a direct debit mandate nominating the account you wish to have your monthly repayments debited from.

Money laundering requirements

Appropriate documentation must be furnished to your lender to satisfy money laundering legislation as set out in section 32 of the Criminal Justice Act 1994. In order to do so your identification must be verified by way of photographic ID such as your passport or drivers licence and you must provide a suitable utility bill in order to verify your present address.

These are standard conditions that will appear with all offer letters, Other frequently appearing conditions are:

Final valuation
If the property you purchased is new and not yet complete, as evidenced by the lender from the initial valuation carried out on your property they will insert a condition in your offer letter that a final valuation be carried out on your property. It will mean sending out the valuer who carried out the first valuation for a second time to ensure the property is complete and habitable. The lender will require confirmation from the valuer in writing that this is the case.

Stage payments
In the case of stage payments you will note a condition in your offer letter stating that your lender will advance funds in 'stages' if you so wish. This is of particular relevance to self-builds or houses purchased in a housing estate requiring stage payments. Upon receiving confirmation and supporting documentation from your supervising architect that the work is completed to a certain stage, and they recommend that a sum of money be released, your lender will furnish the amount requested to your solicitor.

Deed of confirmation
As many borrowers are now receiving gifts from their parents to help fund their purchase, which will normally come in the form of the deposit, lenders will insist that they make a statutory declaration confirming the amount gifted to their son or daughter is in fact a gift and not a loan where they expect to receive back the amount given. A lender will also insist that the donor confirm that they will not acquire any interest in the property by reason of their financial contribution towards its purchase. This legally declared document must be forwarded to the lender before they issue your loan cheque.

Confirmation your existing loan is cleared in full

You may have an existing car or personal loan in place at the time of applying for your loan facility. It may be a condition in your offer that this loan be repaid in full and evidence that this is done be forwarded to your lender before your cheque issues. They may have insisted on this as otherwise you would not have qualified for the amount requested because your existing monthly commitment combined with your new mortgage repayment would have been outside their lending criteria.

As stated previously there may be other conditions in your offer letter that will have to be complied with before a lender will issue your solicitor with a loan cheque, so ensure you read the offer letter and the conditions attaching to it carefully, and if you are unsure about any particular condition be sure to ask your mortgage adviser.

Step 5 (Cheque issue)

Once the conditions that appear on your offer letter are satisfied and the legal documentation that is required from your solicitor is returned and approved by your lender they will furnish your solicitor with your loan cheque.

Normally once a lender is in receipt of everything and checks and verifies that all is in order your solicitor can expect to be in receipt of your loan cheque within the next two or three days.

Once your solicitor receives your cheque they will complete their closing searches. The sale is normally completed at the office of the vendor's solicitor. Your solicitor will pay over the moneys due and will then receive the original title deeds and the keys.

You must call to your solicitor's office to sign the appropriate documentation transferring the title of the property into your name so that you are the legal owner of the property. Your solicitor in turn will send all the title documents to the Land Registry, applying for you to be registered and noted as the owner. They will also apply to have the mortgage registered on the title.

OK, so your loan cheque has issued, when do you start repaying? This will depend on your lender. Some will request the first instalment at the end of the month in which your cheque has issued. However, it will not be a full month's repayment; it will depend on the date the cheque issued and the number of days left in the month. So, for example, if your cheque issued on 20 June your first instalment would be calculated based on the remaining ten days left in the month. Your lender will notify you of this first instalment amount.

Other lenders will not request funds from your account until the following month on the particular date your loan cheque issued. Using the above example: if your cheque issued on 20 June your first full instalment will be due on 20 July.

Some lenders will insist that the mortgage repayment be made on a particular day of the month or give you a choice of repayment dates. As each bank differs just ask your adviser and they will confirm when and how much your first instalment will be. This is actually important as you do not want to get off on the wrong foot with your lender and miss the first repayment!

So after all that you are now the proud owner of your own property – congratulations!

Costs associated with your purchase
Deposit
The majority of lenders will lend a certain percentage of the purchase price of your property. The percentage will vary depending on whether you are a first-time buyer, trading up, non resident or investor.

If you are a first-time buyer a mortgage company will typically lend 92% of the purchase price, so you have to contribute 8% yourself. Let's take an example of this on a property costing €250,000. A lender will advance you €230,000, i.e. 92% of €250,000, so you have to contribute €20,000 from your own funds.

This is quite a substantial sum of money to contribute and it would take some dedication and commitment on your part to save this amount. Some lifestyle changes may have to be made!

Of course many of us who may be currently renting will find it next to impossible to save that amount of money within a reasonable time period and are in a Catch-22 situation: do you continue to rent and try and save your deposit knowing prices are increasing each year or do you continue to rent until your circumstances change for the better – for example your salary increases or you inherit some money.

The other frustrating thing is that many people are paying higher rent each month than what their mortgage repayment would be but the problem is this 8%. Statistics, though, show that one-third of first-time buyers do fund the deposit by way of savings accumulated by them

So what is the solution? You know you need your 8% so you have to either:

- Start saving harder if possible
- Receive a gift of the deposit from a family member

This has become a very common phenomenon nowadays where people are fortunate enough to have parents who will gift them part or all of the 8% required. A lender will be satisfied with this provided the parents make a statutory declaration that following the gift they expect to (a) receive no payment back following the gift and (b) waive their rights to any interest in the property.

100% mortgage
As explained on page 36 this is a new product offering available to first-time buyers. Should you meet the criteria set out by the lender then it would be of great benefit to you in getting on the property ladder without first having to find 8% of the purchase price.

Don't borrow it!
You will note a glaring omission on my part: I do not propose borrowing the 8% as a fourth solution. The reason for this is twofold: one, I don't believe it is a good idea or good advice to go and borrow, for example, €20,000. You will obviously have a financial commitment to repaying this amount back to whatever source you borrowed it from in the first place. This repayment will be a burden to you along with your monthly mortgage repayment. Along with other loans you may have now or take on in the future that personal loan you borrowed for your deposit will weigh most heavily around your neck because from experience it takes a much longer time to repay than you had originally planned on and it is a fact that rather than repay the loan sooner rather than later, people actually top up and increase this loan.

The second reason why it is not a good idea is that lenders frown upon you having to borrow your deposit unless you have a good reason for not having some form of savings. Unless you can clearly demonstrate that you have the capacity to repay your mortgage and deposit loan your chances of securing that mortgage will be seriously jeopardised and your application is likely to be refused.

Legal fees

The role played by your solicitor in your purchase is a very important one and can command a considerable amount of time and energy from them.

When calculating and explaining what your legal fees are going to be, your solicitor may break the cost down into two separate parts. The first is what they will charge you for their own time in carrying out the conveyancing process on your behalf.

This can vary from solicitor to solicitor. Some may charge you a percentage of the purchase price and others may charge you a flat fee irrespective of price. It has become quite competitive now and some solicitors competing for this business will be prepared to negotiate their fee with you to ensure they get your business. Gone are the days of every solicitor charging 1.5% of the purchase price. So before you decide on a solicitor, shop around, get a quotation from a number of firms so you can at least compare prices before deciding on who you are going to proceed with.

It is amazing the number of people who complain about what they were charged in legal fees after their loan cheque completes. So don't be surprised and ask for a quotation so you can budget and prepare for this fee. I assure you a solicitor will not be offended if you ask.

People often refer to how high legal fees are but in fairness to your solicitor they do a considerable amount of work on your behalf, some of which you will never know about.

Whilst price is a very important factor when deciding who is going to act for you, also bear in mind any knowledge you may have of a prospective solicitor's reputations and service. There are times when you will happily pay more for someone whom you have heard good things about or have had good experience with in the past, and of course someone who you trust and feel comfortable with.

Bear in mind that when you are being quoted a fee by a solicitor for their professional time and expertise it may or may not include VAT. More often than not it will but ask nonetheless.

So the first part of your legal bill is made up of your solicitor's own personal fee, plus VAT at 21%.

The second part of your legal bill is referred to as outlay. When your solicitor is in receipt of contracts for the purchase of your new property they will be able to determine where the title of the property is held, that is either with the Land Registry or the Registry of Deeds. The cost applicable to your 'outlay' will depend on which one.

When I refer to title I am talking about the legal documents that prove ownership of the property.

If the title of the property is held with the Registry of Deeds the following fees will apply:

Registration of a Deed of Conveyance	€44.00
Registration of a Mortgage	€44.00
Registration of a Vacate (removing a previous mortgage)	€12.00
If the title of the property is Land Registry then the following will apply:	
Registration of mortgage	€125.00
Registration of ownership:	
The following fees will apply on all transfers of sale	
where the value of consideration is:	
€1–13,000	€125.00
€13,301–26,000	€190.00
€26,601–51,000	€250.00
€51,001–255,000	€375.00
€255,001–385,000	€500.00
€385,001+	€625.00

So if you are a first-time buyer or, for that matter, a second-time buyer purchasing a new property for which stage payments are required it would be usual for the purchase of the site to be included with the first stage payment. If this is the case the fees outlined above will apply. So if the overall purchase price of your property is, for example, €300,000 but the site cost €25,000 to purchase, a fee of €190.00 will apply.

If you are not purchasing the site initially or, for example, the property is second-hand the fees above will apply on the full purchase price, so using the same example above – a purchase price of €300,000 – now your registration of ownership or deed of transfer fee will be €500.00. A big difference!

Other fees will include:

Land certificate	€25.00
Certificate of charge	€6.00
Copy folio	€25.00

Search fees

These fees can vary dramatically depending on the type of transaction and company that is carrying out the searches. If you are purchasing in a new development, for example, a company search on the builder will be required in addition to judgement, bankruptcy and Land Registry searches. All these can make the search fees much higher. Furthermore, one company may own the land and another may develop it so two company searches would be required.

If stage payments are required a search will have to be carried out at each stage, making the search fees more expensive again, depending on the number of stage payments required.

Stamp duty on mortgage deed

Loans in excess of €254,000 will attract a stamp duty rate of 0.1%. This rate applies to the total amount once it is over €254,000, with the maximum chargeable at €630.00.

For example if you were to take out a mortgage of €280,000 to enable you to purchase a property the stamp duty on the mortgage deed would be €280.00, i.e. €280,000 x 0.1%.

Assignment of life policy

Many lenders will require that the life policy effected by you be assigned to them as security. There will be a flat fee of €12.50 should the mortgage exceed €254,000.

Administrative expenses

Outlay with regard to postage, telephone and fax charges can vary greatly depending on the amount of work required.

So all of the above will form part of the outlay fee in your overall legal bill.

Next to follow in your house-buying costs are:

Structural survey

If you are purchasing a property either for use as your main residence or for investment purposes it would be prudent first to have a structural report carried out it.

The function of such a survey is to examine and evaluate the current condition of the property and highlight any defects or repairs that will need attention now or in the future.

The report can be very detailed and comprehensive and will be carried out by a qualified architect or engineer.

A lender will not insist on a structural report on the property they are mortgaging – that is unless it is of a certain age – so the decision to get one carried out is completely yours.

Expect to pay a fee of between €300 and €500 for such a report but the peace of mind it will give you will mean it is money well spent.

Valuation fee

A lender will insist that a valuation is carried out on the property they are providing funds for. This valuation differs from a structural report as it is very much a superficial inspection examining the interior and exterior of the property.

The lender requires this type of valuation so they can get independent confirmation from a third party as to what the current market value of the property is.

The report will also highlight to the lender details such as:

- Description of the property and its approximate age
- Services such as water, electricity and gas
- If currently under construction, what stage the property is at and the estimated date of completion
- Size of the property
- Number of rooms in the property

- Market value
- Recommended reinstatement value for insurance purposes
- Estimated rental income from the property each month
- Valuer's signature and name and address of the firm

The fee for this initial valuation will range between €130 and €180, depending on the location of the property.

If the property is under construction a second final valuation will be required and will be carried out by the valuer who did the original inspection. The cost for this final valuation will typically be €70.

Indemnity bond fee

This is a fee that may apply if you are borrowing above a certain percentage of the property's value. It insures your lender in the event of your defaulting on the loan.

This premium, if applicable, will be repaid prior to your mortgage closing.

This form of insurance covers the lender only and offers no protection to you, the borrower.

As the mortgage market is very competitive at the moment the majority of lenders do not charge this fee any longer but ask and make sure it does not apply to you.

Stamp-duty costs

First-time buyers were delighted in December 2004 when Minister of Finance Brian Cowen announced that he was abolishing stamp duty on many second-hand properties.

Previously first-time buyers who were purchasing a second-hand property valued between €190,501 and €254,000 had to pay 3% on the purchase price and 3.75% on properties between €254,000 and €317,500. This was a significant additional cost that the purchaser had to incur and depending on the purchase price could have been as high as €11,000.

Now first-time buyers can buy a second-hand property up to a purchase price of €317,500 without paying any stamp duty, and homes from €317,500 to €635,000 will benefit from reduced levels.

This was very good news for first-time buyers as it increased the choice of property available to them; many had previously limited their search to new developments as there was (and is) no stamp duty payable on a new property for first-time buyers.

The abolition of stamp duty for first-time buyers up to this new threshold of €317,500 has attracted new purchasers to the market as the previous stamp-duty rates meant that many first-time buyers could simply not afford to buy into the second-hand market. Their outlay was just too much, given that they had to contribute 8% themselves towards the purchase, pay legal fees and furnish the house. The extra €5,000 to €10,000 for stamp duty, depending on the cost of the property, made a second-hand property just too expensive for many people. The result was that almost half of all new homes were bought by first-time buyers.

So with many second-hand properties now being seriously considered by first-time buyers it may mean better deals for buyers in new developments as builders will recognise that first-timers now do not have to consider only new properties. This may result in increased competition amongst builders who may offer incentives to new purchasers as part of their package.

The stamp duty now applicable for first-time buyers is:

Up to €317,500	Exempt
€317,501 – 381,000	3%
€381,001 – 635,000	6%
€635,001+	9%

If first-time buyers are purchasing a new property or apartment and it is under 125 square metres, no stamp duty is payable regardless of the purchase price. If the property is over 125 square metres, the stamp duty rates apply but the market value for stamp duty purposes is calculated as either (a) site value or (b) a quarter of the overall cost, whichever of the two is greater. Therefore for a first-time buyer the cost of a new house would in general need to be over €1,270,000 before stamp duty arises i.e. 25% of €1,270,000 = €317,500.

Should you purchase a property where the purchase price is inclusive of some contents this can be taken into account for the purpose of determining the rate band that will be applicable to a residential property. For example, if you were purchasing a property for €350,000 and you were a first-time buyer, and €5,000 of the purchase price was for say carpets, curtains and furniture, the stamp duty would be calculated on the purchase price minus the cost of the contents i.e. €345,000.

If you were to receive a gift of a site or were sold a property at a reduced price by a relative you might be liable for stamp duty. For example, if a mother were to sell a property to her daughter (let's assume her daughter is single and a first-time buyer) for €400,000 but the market value of the property is in fact €500,000 her daughter would be liable for stamp duty at a rate of 6% of the market value of the property i.e. €30,000. However, this rate can be reduced by half by availing of a relief known as 'Consanguinity Relief' which applies when the sale or transfer of a property is between certain specified relatives. So, availing of this relief in this example would reduce the stamp duty implication by half from €30,000 to €15,000.

Your status – whether you are a first-time or second-time buyer, your marital status and the relationship of the person or persons receiving the site or property at a reduced price – will have a bearing on whether you can avail of this Consanguinity Relief. Using the example above, if you were to purchase a property for €400,000 from your mother but the property was worth €500,000 and you were married and not a first-time buyer you and your husband or wife would be liable for stamp duty at the full rate i.e. 7.5% of €500,000 = €37,500.

Finally, a very important point to note is that if the property you purchased ceases to be your private residence and is let out by you within five years from the date you bought it a clawback on stamp duty may arise. The Revenue will impose stamp duty on the amount that would have arisen had the property been let from the time it was purchased. Allowance for the time you spent in the property may be taken into account.

Stamp duty position for joint applicants where one is a first-time buyer and the other is not

It is very common nowadays for a first-time buyer to have an additional borrower or guarantor join with them in a mortgage for the purpose of securing the amount required as they may not have qualified based on their single income alone.

This created a situation with regard to exemption from stamp duty. According to the Revenue, in order to qualify for this relief all the funds borrowed and any other funds used to purchase must be provided by the first-time buyer. Any other person who is party to providing money or is jointly borrowing money that is going to be used for a house purchase will also be regarded as a buyer of the property and stamp-duty relief will not be available unless that other person is a first-time buyer. This ruling will apply even if the person recorded in the deeds is the first-time buyer.

This has obviously created a problem for many first-time buyers who may have been lucky enough to have had family support in assisting them with, for example, their deposit or where a father or mother were prepared to join with their son or daughter in the mortgage for the purpose of helping them secure a property for themselves. It is hard enough to get approval based on one income to buy a property in the development or area you wish to purchase in and after saving as much as you could now to be faced with the possibility of having to pay stamp duty just because, for example, your father gave you a gift of €10,000 towards the purchase or acted as guarantor with your mortgage is very galling.

However the Revenue have taken this situation into account and are now prepared to accept that a first-time buyer will not have to pay stamp duty if their parents gift them money towards the purchase or act as co-mortgagers provided the following conditions are satisfied:

- The transfer of the house is taken in the name of the first-time buyer.
- It is the intention of the first-time buyer and the parent that the parent should have no beneficial interest in the property.
- The parent has joined in on the mortgage at the request of the lending institution in order to secure the funds required as the first-time buyer would not have otherwise qualified for the amount needed.
- The repayments will be met solely by the first-time buyer and the parent will not be contributing to the repayment of the mortgage.

If the above conditions are satisfied the Revenue will treat the parent as effectively acting in the role of guarantor for the loan so no stamp-duty implication will befall the first-time buyer.

Revenue have also decided that any persons other than parents of the first-time buyer who satisfy the conditions as outlined above will also be acting as so their involvement in this capacity will not preclude a claim to the first-time buyer relief.

I suggest, though, that you speak to your solicitor and get expert legal advice from them if this is relevant to your particular situation.

Tax relief for home-loan interest

Tax relief for home-loan interest is available in respect of a person's sole or main residence i.e. the house we own.

First-time buyers are entitled to greater relief than is generally allowed for payment of home-loan interest. The Revenue considers a first-time buyer as an individual who has not been entitled to claim relief up to this. The increased relief lasts for a period of seven years before it falls back to the general level.

Therefore the maximum allowable in interest relief for married first-time buyers is €8,000, for single/separated/divorced first-time buyers is €4,000 and for widowed buyers is €8,000 per annum. These limits are calculated at a tax rate of 20% so for example the maximum tax saving for a married first-time buyer would be €1,600 per annum i.e. €8,000 x 20%.

Mortgage interest relief for non-first-time buyers on residential property occupied as their main private residence is again calculated at the standard rate of tax – i.e. 20% – and the limits are: single/separated/divorced €2,540, married couple €5,080 and widowed €5,080.

Status	Maximum allowance at standard rate for first time buyers	Maximum tax credit for first time buyers per annum	Maximum allowance at standard rate for non-first time buyers	Maximum tax relief for non-first time buyers per annum
Married	€8,000	€1,600	€5,080	€1,016
Single	€4,000	€800	€2,540	€508
Widowed	€8,000	€1,600	€5,080	€1,016

Bridging loan interest

Tax relief is allowed for interest paid for a bridging loan facility used to finance the purchase of a property before your existing property is sold. The relief is limited to a maximum period of 12 months from the date the loan is issued. The relief is subject to the same restrictions as mortgage interest is but you can claim relief on both loans at the same time.

Tax relief at source

Since 1 January 2002 the method by which mortgage interest relief is granted has been changed. Now your mortgage provider will give the benefit on the interest paid by you. This was previously granted by the Revenue. Your lender will in turn claim this relief given by them back from the Revenue.

What this means now is that your mortgage repayment will effectively be reduced by the tax relief amount. The amount of relief will, depending on your lender, be credited to your mortgage account each month.

You will receive a tax relief at source form from the lender providing you with the mortgage and you complete the relevant details on same and return for processing to the Revenue.

4
Building a Property

What your mortgage lender will look for!

When you are looking to borrow moneys to fund the purchase of a site and also the funds to build on it, there is a number of considerations you should be aware of from the start, in terms of what a bank will require and also what you are likely to encounter.

First of all, a lender will want answers from you to a number of questions apart from the usual income, employment and savings. These are: What is the site cost? What is the likely cost to build? Is there full planning permission granted for the type and size of house you wish to build? Are you building by direct labour or by way of registered builder? If building by registered builder, is there a fixed price contract? Who is going to supervise the construction of the property and are they suitably qualified and bonded? How many stage payments do you estimate you will require?

Stage payments mean that the mortgage can be drawn down in a number of amounts over a period of time rather than in one amount on closing. This is to assist people who are building a house or are having one built by a builder. There are typically four stages: foundations, roof, plastering and on completion. The monthly repayments to the lender are calculated on the amount currently drawn down and not the overall mortgage amount.

The amount advanced to people buying a site and building for owner occupation is normally 92% of the value of the property on completion, assuming they will qualify for the amount requested. However, the amount advanced for site purchase will typically be a maximum of 85% of the cost of the site, providing full planning permission is in place or if alternative security is offered if outline or no planning permission exists. Evidence must also be provided to a lender that the applicant intends to commence development of the site within a six-month period, i.e. a building contract needs to be signed/agreed.

Finally, some factors that you should also bear in mind are:

- Legal costs
- Planning costs
- Supervising architect's costs
- Insurance in the course of construction
- Fitting out and finishing
- Approach drive, fences, gates and landscaping
- Connection to utilities
- Alternative accommodation expenses

Did you know?

- Since December 2000 a parent can transfer land owned by them into their children's name without being liable for capital gains tax when the reason for transferring the land in the first place was to allow their child to build their private residence on the land and providing the market value of the land does not exceed €254,000.

A self-build property is often viewed by lenders as a proposition they have to examine very closely and be comfortable financing.

There is a number of considerations that have to be taken into account by the lender before agreeing to finance the cost to build. Their worst-case scenario is that the borrower has either under-estimated the cost required to build the property and runs short of funds to complete or abandons the build altogether half-way through, leaving a lender with half a house to repossess and sell.

So even if repayment capacity is not a problem, a lender will have to be satisfied that:

- Full planning permission exists and the property built complies with the conditions as laid out in the planning permission.
- The property will have appropriate access and rights of way.
- The construction of the property is supervised by a qualified architect/engineer.

- The property when completed is fully serviced with water, electricity etc.
- The property is completed within a certain time period as delays may push up costs.

As stated previously the maximum a lender will normally advance with full planning permission in place is 85% of the site cost, so you will initially be contributing 15% of your own funds towards the site purchase.

Thereafter the amount required will be released in 'stage payments'. Your supervising architect/engineer will confirm and provide evidence to your lender that the property has reached a certain stage and been completed satisfactorily. They will recommend that the lender release x amount to you. They will further advise what has been spent to date on the construction of the property.

Your architect/engineer plays a very important role for you and your lender. Before a lender will advance any moneys or indeed give you a letter of loan offer, they must first be satisfied that your architect/engineer is qualified to carry out the inspections and furthermore require written confirmation from them that they will:

- Supervise the construction of the property
- Confirm whether the property is being build by direct labour or by way of fixed-price contract
- Confirm that they supervised the open foundations and certify that they are satisfactory
- On completion of the property, furnish the lender with a certificate of compliance confirming compliance with planning and building regulations
- They will also have to confirm that they hold professional indemnity insurance and furnish the lender with a copy of same

Stamp duty for purchase of a site with no building agreement in place

Where a site is purchased but you do not have any building agreement in place for the construction of a property that will be used as your private home the site is considered non-residential property and stamp duty will apply, depending on the price paid. This is a very important point to note.

The payment of stamp duty will apply even if it was always your intention to build and you subsequently do build your own property on the site.

Below are the stamp duty rates applicable for non-residential property

Up to €10,000	Exempt
€10,001–20,000	1%
€20,001–30,000	2%
€30,001–40,000	3%
€40,001–70,000	4%
€70,001–80,000	5%
€80,001–100,000	6%
€100,001–120,000	7%
€120,001–150,000	8%
Over €150,001	9%

The table above will also apply to property that is purchased that will not be occupied as a private residence by you or others. It is most applicable for the purchase of commercial premises or land, including sites.

Direct labour
This term refers to those who are building a property and who arrange for plasterers, bricklayers, plumbers and so on to carry out specific work on their property.

When this is the case, lenders have to be very comfortable that you have costed the amount required in detail and will make it clear that the amount offered in the offer letter is final so you have to come in on budget.

The advantage of building a property by direct labour is that your property can be built much more cheaply especially if you have knowledge of the building trade yourself and know tradesmen who can assist you.

The big disadvantages, though, are the potential cost overruns so be very detailed and precise when budgeting for what is required and always allow for that little bit more – it may come in handy!

Fixed price contract

This is where you enter into an agreement with a registered builder that they will construct your property as outlined in the plans/specifications you provided to them for a fixed agreed fee.

Lenders have more of a comfort here in that the potential for overruns is eliminated by agreement to the fixed-price contract. They will, however, still require that you retain an architect/engineer to supervise the construction of the property and the documentation required is the same as if it were direct labour.

It will be specified in the contract with your builder and agreed by you that, for example, €30,000 is provided to your builder when foundations are poured, a further €30,000 released when wall-plate level is reached, and these amounts may be specified in your offer letter, depending on the lender.

The advantage of using a registered builder is that you should know the quality of their workmanship. having viewed previous properties built by them before deciding to employ them. At least this is what you *should* do. You then have a comfort knowing that your property is being built by qualified, experienced professionals. You also have a comfort knowing that the price agreed will complete your property to the level stipulated in your building agreement and generally you can expect the property to be completed within an agreed time-frame.

When sourcing a builder you should get a minimum of three quotations from potential builders so you can compare the cost. You could be surprised by how much they differ. The one disadvantage to proceeding this way is actually finding a builder who is available, one who is within your price range and finally one who is ready to start your property after you give them reasonable notice.

One other important factor to consider when selecting your builder is whether they are registered under Homebond or not. This leads me nicely to:

What is HomeBond Insurance?

HomeBond was set up in the late 1970s with government approval. It was designed to provide a regulatory framework for the private-housing building sector. Over 2000 builders are currently registered within the scheme. HomeBond specifies that properties are constructed to a very high standard and they will periodically inspect properties being built to ensure compliance to HomeBond's Standards of Construction.

This is a service provided by the National House Building Guarantee Company Ltd. Owners of all newly-built homes whose builders are members of the HomeBond scheme have cover which:

- Guarantees home against major structural defects for ten years
- Guarantees home against water and smoke penetration for the first two years
- Guarantees cover against the loss of stage payments before the new house is completed

If the registered builder is declared bankrupt or goes into liquidation HomeBond will repay the purchaser's deposit or contract payments up to a maximum of 15% of the purchase price or €25,400, whichever is the lower. This provision will operate from the date of registration with HomeBond and last for up to two years.

If a dispute or claim is made and either the buyer or builder does not agree with HomeBond's findings, provision is made for independent arbitration. HomeBond does not affect the contractual and common-law rights of the home buyer against the builder. It will give the home buyer additional protection against builders who do not respond to their legitimate complaints. If the owner sells the property within the warranty period, the new purchaser will be covered, provided any defects in the property were not obvious to the new purchaser at the time of the purchase.

Planning permission

If you are going to build a house in Ireland you will first need to obtain full planning permission from your local authority to do so.

Before you make an application for planning it would be prudent to check with your local authority first to view their plan for the area where you wish to build. A plan developed by your local authority will exist, setting out what they want to use particular areas for, such as specific areas targeted for industrial, agricultural or residential use.

Consulting with your local authority will assist you greatly with your application: as well giving you general advice on how to apply, documents required and so on, they will be able to tell you if the property you are looking to build will comply with their development plan for the area.

Before you make an application, there are some points worth noting:

According to the local authority development plan what is planned for the future for the area in which you are proposing to build?

Consult with the planning department in your local authority prior to designing your dream home as the department can guide you on the type of property that may or may not be allowed. You may be disappointed if you have gone to the trouble and expense of designing a three-storey property if you are then told that only bungalow-type properties are acceptable.

When you are getting your house designed be aware of the impact it may have on the area and surrounding environment. The planning department will look at this closely before granting permission.

Before you apply for planning permission seek expert advice from a qualified architect or engineer.

Planning permission process

Prior to making an application for planning permission you have to give public notice of your intentions.

This is done by erecting a site notice that is clearly visible and can be clearly read. Information that will appear in this notice will be in a prescribed format, as outlined in the application form. You will also have to place your proposed notice and intention in a locally circulated newspaper. Your local authority will advise you as to what newspapers are acceptable to them.

Your planning application has to be with your local authority for consideration within two weeks of the notice appearing in your local newspaper. The site notice must also be on display on or before the date your application is submitted and must remain on site for at least one month.

Your local authority has to make a decision on your application within eight weeks of receiving it. However it may request additional information from you, which can lengthen the decision-making process.

When your local authority makes a decision about your application and it is successful, you will be given a notice of intention to grant you planning permission.

If no one objects to or appeals against the planning permission granted within one month of the date of the decision you will get a grant of permission from your local authority.

You must not start building your property until you receive your grant of permission.

Full planning permission will typically last for a five-year period.

If your application for planning permission is refused by your local authority you can appeal the decision to An Bord Pleanála.

Your appeal must be in writing and made within four weeks from the date of the decision made by the planning department of your local authority.

There are three main types of planning permission:

Outline planning permission
This is sought when you are going to build a property in the near future but you have not decided on, for example, its design. You may also just not be ready personally to commence building your property.

When applying for this type of permission, although you may not have a specific design or specification in mind at the moment, you will have to advise, for example, whether the property is going to be one- or two-storey building; if it is going to have a septic tank or a bio-waste treatment; and the layout of the site on which the property is going to be built. This will assist the local authority in making its decision.

Normally outline planning permission will last for a period of three years.

Permission following the grant of outline planning permission
This is applied for when you are ready to go ahead with your
proposed design and you have all the documentation needed for full
planning permission.

Full planning permission
You apply for full planning permission when you have decided on
all your plans/designs and if this is approved you are ready to start
construction straight away.

Documents required when applying for planning permission
- Six copies of the application form, completed in full and
  signed by you
- Six copies of an ordnance survey map showing the location
  of the site
- Six copies of the site or layout plan
- Six copies of detailed structural drawings and specifications
  of the proposed development
- The original page of the newspaper containing the notice
  together with an additional five copies of same and six copies
  of the site notice
- A fee, which is currently €65
- If applicable, six copies of a suitability report detailing trail
  hole and percolation test results carried out within the last 12
  months by a qualified person holding adequate professional
  indemnity insurance

5
Remortgaging

Is now the best time to remortgage?

The past number of years has seen a significant number of people remortgaging and I expect this trend to continue for the foreseeable future. Fears that interest rates may rise in the coming months and years have led to understandable concern over the affordability of mortgages alongside other debts. People are also becoming increasingly aware of the benefits of remortgaging as they see it is a way to help them manage all their finances.

Psychologically, the New Year is always a good time to review your personal finances but from a mortgage point of view, you should really focus on whether your current mortgage suits your needs. Even if you think you are getting a good rate, it is well worth taking a look at your mortgage as you can only benefit from the exercise and also give yourself peace of mind.

It is amazing how little attention people pay to their mortgage once they have arranged it and is in force. Many times people complain when they see the rates on offer to new borrowers and feel aggrieved that as an existing customer the same rate is not offered to them. The answer to this frustration may lie with remortgaging.

It is common nowadays for many people to have a number of repayments each month going towards servicing loans they have taken out with banks, building societies or credit unions, The reason for the loans will vary depending on the person and their circumstances at the time of taking out the loan but their purpose will typically be a mortgage, a car loan, a personal loan, a holiday loan or credit card repayments.

Your monthly repayment will depend on the type of loan you

have, the term chosen and the rate offered. Obviously the longest term at the lowest rate available will result in the lowest monthly premium for you on the amount borrowed.

The purpose of the loan in the first place and the security on offer will have an effect on the term and rate offered. For example, borrowing funds to purchase a property can be arranged for a term up to your 70th birthday with rates from as low as 2.74%. A lender has a comfort that, based on your present and future earnings, you can repay the loan they advanced you and a worst-case scenario that if you are unable to meet the repayments they have a property they can repossess and sell to recoup any moneys owed.

If you borrow funds to buy a car, the rate offered will normally depend on how much you are borrowing against the actual value of the car and the term, which will be based on the age of the car. The rate offered to those who are maybe borrowing only 50% of the value of the car will typically be less than if someone was trying to finance the full purchase price as the risk perceived by the lender is less and the lower rate rewarded to those who are considered less of a risk.

Why remortgage?

You could remortgage for a couple of reasons. The first reason is to switch from your current provider to another who is offering you a better rate. The rate reduction would have to justify the switch when legal fees are taken into account as well as the possible long-term savings you may achieve. It is common nowadays for lenders to offer to pay your legal fees if you switch your mortgage to them. When people do explore the idea of remortgaging in order to reduce the rate of interest they pay, some may feel that it is not be worth the hassle when they discover that they will save maybe only €30 each month. Sure, the difference isn't life-changing now but over a 20-year period on a loan amount of €100,000 you would save nearly €7,500, or have your mortgage cleared off 13 months earlier! Would you prefer to give your bank an extra €7,500? If so, fair enough; they will gladly accept it from you.

The number of people who are currently repaying at least 0.5% more than what they could be repaying is staggering – and whose fault is it but their own? Do *you* know what your mortgage rate is?

The second and more popular reason for remortgaging is debt-

consolidation. That is the grouping together of all your loans into
one loan with one monthly repayment. This can be done if you have
sufficient equity in your property so that (a) there are enough funds
available to clear off the remaining balances owed on your other
loans and (b) there is sufficient comfort from a lender's point of
view that you can repay this new increased amount – which, don't
forget, will be secured on your private residence. Also they will not
want to be overexposed on the amount advanced against the value of
the security they have. Normally a lender will not advance more than
90% of the value of your property for remortgaging with many only
advancing up to 85%. So, assuming your house is valued at €200,000
you could remortgage up to a maximum of €180,000, i.e. 90% of
€200,000.

As a quick example, here are the details of a remortgage I did
recently for clients who were repaying the following:

Loan	Amount outstanding	Monthly repayment
Mortgage	€50,000	€397
Credit Card	€7,000	€350
Car Loan	€12,000	€248
Credit Union Loan	€6,000	€294
Total	€75,000	€1,289

Their existing mortgage was at a variable rate of 3.6% and they had a
13-year term left on it.

Their monthly outgoings were high and whilst they could afford
the repayments it did not leave a lot left over each month. So I
arranged a remortgage for them whereby we consolidated all their
loans into one and now they have:

Loan	Amount outstanding	Monthly repayment
Mortgage	€75,000	€724.50

They improved their cashflow by €565.50 per month. Now the
savings achieved can be put to use: portions will go towards a regular
savings plan, a pension plan and that holiday they always wanted.
However, the best thing that happened was not only the monthly

saving but a reduction of three years in the term of their mortgage.

When you are taking over short-term debt it is very important to be aware of the fact that you could be financing that car or personal loan over a much longer period that you had initially anticipated. Your total repayments are reduced because you are financing them over a 15- or 20-year term at home-loan rates. The advantage to structuring your debt this way is that you are improving your cashflow considerably. You also have the option, when remortgaging, of structuring your loan in such a way that the car loan you consolidated with your mortgage is still repaid over a three- or four-year period. The cashflow savings will then not be so great but it is an option available to you which you should explore. Compare both options and decide which one suits your present circumstances best.

Another benefit of remortgaging is the ability to reduce the duration of your loan. With extra money each month and more flexible products now available such as the mortgage current account, it is possible to overpay your mortgage loan and pay it off early without incurring any redemption penalties.

By remortgaging you can also release equity built up in your house. By remortgaging for a sum that is greater than the amount needed to repay the original mortgage, you can release money to purchase a new car, make DIY improvements or invest in a second home.

When people think of remortgaging, the very thought of it conjures up images of financial strife, but nothing could be further from the reality. Remortgaging can be a very positive experience. Yes, there can be set-up costs (although some lenders are now paying the legal fees incurred if you switch your mortgage to them) but as shown above, massive savings can be achieved. Although the process of remortgaging is similar to getting a normal mortgage, it is faster as you are not buying a home. Depending on the lender, it takes around five to six weeks. If you need to remortgage fast, some lenders offer fast-track services that can complete in as little as ten days, but it does depend on individual circumstances.

When deciding whether to remortgage or not, you need to think about what you get out of your current mortgage as well as what you want from a new product. These are some of the questions you should ask yourself:

- What are my current repayments and am I able to lower these?
- Can I get a better deal from my existing lender?
- Does my rate still meet my requirements, e.g. fixed or variable?
- What costs are involved?
- Am I saving enough to justify remortgaging?
- Does my existing mortgage have any redemption penalties?

Do you know?

- What your current mortgage rate is? And is there a better rate out there that is available to you that could help reduce your monthly repayments or accelerate the repayment of your mortgage?
- Remortgaging can help save your cashflow situation by consolidating a number of loans into one monthly repayment at home-loan rates.
- You may have to pay fees for switching so check how much these are likely to be or check with a lender to see if they will pay your legal fees for switching to them
- The maximum any lender will advance on a remortgage is 90% of the current value of your home.

What is equity release?

Equity-release mortgages have been around for some time but the comforting thing about them is that they have, like many other things in life, improved with age.

Many people today find themselves with a valuable asset in their home and have limited income to support their wishes and achieve the ambitions which are yet to be fulfilled. The solution may simply be to consider releasing an acceptable percentage equity value on your home and realising this as capital to be used and employed as you wish.

Equity is the difference between the current value of your property and the amount of mortgage that is outstanding on your home. For example, if you purchased a property five years ago for €150,000 and you borrowed €100,000, the equity in the property was €50,000. If the same property is now valued at €200,000 and the mortgage has reduced to €90,000 the equity in the property is now €110,000.

Many people who in the past would have considered trading up to a bigger property are now availing of an equity-release type loan to build an extension or renovate their existing home rather than moving. When they look at the costs of selling and buying, together with the emotional costs of leaving, they realise that doing up or extending their existing home is another option available to them.

Equity release from your property can provide funding for the following purposes:

- Release money from your property to consolidate debts
- Equity release from your property can help you buy a holiday home
- Home improvements – further increase the value of your property
- Raise capital from your house for special occasions e.g. a wedding
- Remortgage your home for that dream holiday/car

Equity release or remortgaging is now a well recognised way for parents to help their children to buy a first home. Releasing money to 'gift' to your children to cover their deposit, solicitor fees, stamp duty (if applicable) is becoming more and more popular.

In all applications for equity release, the bank will require up-to-date income certificates and property valuation as well as increased life and property insurance. Additional legal costs may be incurred to secure extra borrowing.

Home-improvement loans
Many home-improvement projects begin with someone in the household saying, 'Wouldn't it be nice ...?' What follows may be a wish for a new kitchen/bathroom or an extension with space to accommodate every family member's needs. However, reality usually intrudes upon this daydream: you only have so much money and so much space. So how do you turn your dreams into reality? Start by assessing your needs. Most homeowners consider home improvements for one of the following reasons.

You need to update the out-of-date. If your kitchen still has appliances and decor from decades past, now may be the time to make it up to date and modern.

You need to replace fixtures or appliances. Sometimes a home-improvement project grows out of an immediate need to replace broken or inefficient fixtures. If the bath, shower or toilet needs to be replaced, many people take the opportunity to refurbish the entire bathroom.

You're selling your home. You want to be sure you'll get the best price from the sale of your home, and that may be the rallying cry for some home-improvement projects.

You're staying put. You thought about moving, but now you realise that improving your present home is a better option.

Your family has grown and you need more space.

Before you decide that you are going to embark on your home-improvement project you need to start doing some research of your own. How much is it going to cost? Try and be as exact as possible to avoid overruns and maybe budget for that extra unforeseen €1,000 or €2,000. How much per month is it going to cost you? Find out what, for example, €10,000 is going to cost you on a monthly basis and decide whether this increased repayment is within your budget.

You will also need to find out whether you will require planning permission if you are carrying out an extension to your property. If your improvements are structural, who will carry out the improvements? When you are sourcing a building contractor to carry out the work, ideally you should (a) compare at least three quotes from different builders as prices quoted may differ quite substantially and (b) view some work the builder you have selected has done before. You would certainly want to see the quality of their workmanship before you decide to employ them. Of course the other consideration here is timing. How long will it take before they start and how long will it take them to finish because be sure that work being carried out is going to be an inconvenience for everyone in the home.

Finance for your project by way of borrowing can come from a number of different sources and you want to select the most cost-efficient way possible for you. If you have sufficient equity in your property you could elect to borrow the funds required by way of an equity release-type loan from your existing lender. Here your lender will advance you the sum of money required at home-loan rates provided you meet the normal income criteria and the combined loan to value does not exceed between 80% and 90% of the value of the property.

You could also elect to 'switch' from your current lender to a different one if, for example, the rate on offer from another institution is more competitive. Here your new lender will advance sufficient funds to you which will (a) take over your existing mortgage and (b) the remainder can be used towards your renovations. Looking at repayments and rates for your extension can be a great exercise as you will now be looking at your current mortgage and its competitiveness. You would be surprised when comparing the different rates and products currently on offer at the savings per month you could achieve.

Planning permission for home improvements

If you are considering borrowing funds for the purpose of extending your current property or altering it in any way you may have to obtain planning permission to do this.

Before you start to build an extension or conservatory or convert your garage or outbuilding, check first with your local authority to see if you need planning permission as it is an offence to carry out any work on your property if you do not have planning approval. If you proceed without planning permission and planning permission is required, you could incur a large fine and/or imprisonment and you will be required to demolish your unauthorised extension or conversion.

There are times when no planning permission will be required but as every extension or alteration will differ you should consult with the planning department of your local authority for their advice before proceeding.

However, if you are carrying out the following alterations planning permission is probably not required:

- Converting a garage to the side or rear of your property for domestic use. It must have a floor area less than 40 sq metres.
- Constructing a garage to the side or rear of your property which does not exceed four metres in height. The floor area has to be under 25 sq metres for planning permission exemption and if built on the side of your house it must not extend beyond the building line of your property.
- Building a front porch as long as it is not greater than two sq metres in area and is more than two metres from a public road or footpath. Depending on its roof type it cannot exceed a height of between three and four metres.
- Building gates to your property provided they are not greater than two metres in height.
- Building an extension to the rear of your property not greater in size than 40 sq metres and no higher than your existing house. It is worth noting that after your extension is completed the open space at the rear of your property should not be less than 25 sq metres in area.

The above is just a brief outline of projects that may be exempt from planning permission but, as stated previously, you should consult with your local authority before you undertake any work.

Bear in mind that if your proposed extension or change to your existing property fundamentally changes part or all of your building from residential use to, for example, business use – such as will occur if you convert your garage to a workshop for a business or you start operating a crèche from your home – planning permission will most likely be required.

Tax relief

Tax relief for home-loan interest is available in respect of a person's sole or main residence.

The conditions to qualify for this relief are based upon interest paid on borrowed moneys used for the purchase, repair or improvement to your principal private residence within certain limits (see page 64).

So if you are remortgaging for the purpose of consolidating debts the amount you can claim for will have to be based specifically on the amount borrowed and used for the purchase, repair or improvement of your home. You cannot, therefore, claim this relief on loans such as personal or car loans that were consolidated in your remortgage amount.

6
Buy to Let

Buying a property for investment

As interest rates have fallen in recent years, there has been a boom in the number of people buying property to let out in order to earn a rental income plus the prospect of capital gain.

Everyone knows that property prices have risen substantially over the past number of years and although there have been times when prices in some areas remained stagnant the fact is that the overall trend has been upwards. This means that property is an area that should be considered as an investment opportunity.

As with any investment, you must be cautious. Careful research is needed along with an awareness of the possible pitfalls. The property market in most parts of the country has been and is buoyant at the moment and the prospects are healthy, so for those with the necessary funds and enthusiasm there is no doubt this could prove a rewarding avenue to explore. There has also been fierce competition amongst lenders in this niche market, resulting in highly competitive mortgage rates for those looking to buy property to let.

Your choice of investment property will be based upon the level of rental income you can demand, whether you need a property that offers capital allowances and of course the potential for increase in capital value. As auctioneers say, the three most important factors when choosing a property are location, location, location. The area in which the house is situated will determine the price, the rent and indeed the type of tenant you are likely to attract.

Over the past number of years, many people have viewed property investment as an alternative pension scheme. Although property does not offer the same tax relief as a pension does, people have been put off pension investment due to uncertainty about how their pension fund has been performing and also the large premiums they have to pay to get any sort of a reasonable pension when they do retire. What property does offer is long-term capital growth and some income, particularly once the mortgage has been repaid.

Buying property can be a wise investment but it is important that you do the right research beforehand. That said, with the right property this can be a very rewarding investment opportunity.

Factors to consider before making a decision to purchase an investment property

- You are going to become a landlord and will have to deal with your tenants and the issues that may come with that.
- Do you have the ability to meet the mortgage repayments if the property was unoccupied for a number of months?
- Is the basis for your purchase the projected rental income you have been told you will receive if you buy? No harm in getting a number of opinions from sources other than the selling agent of the property.
- Be aware of possible tax obligations arising from your purchase.
- Are you using your family home as additional collateral with your lender in order to purchase your investment property?
- Is there a demand for rental accommodation in the area you are considering purchasing in?
- What are the advantages of purchasing in the area you are considering and are there any negative factors you should consider? What is the resaleability of properties like in the area at the moment?
- Look at your cashflow situation, factoring in your mortgage repayments, annual running costs, your rental income, your tax liability (if any), interest deductibility etc. and see what the property is going to cost you personally each year. Does it make economic sense to purchase?
- Allowing for your income and expenditure, what return are you achieving based on the property's value each year?
- Are you going to find tenants and collect rent yourself or are you going to let a management company do this for you?

- What are the local amenities like in the area in which you are considering purchasing?
- How safe is the area?
- Is the property located near public transport?
- Is it better to buy an apartment or a house?
- Who are you going to get to draw up your lease agreement?
- Are you going to make your annual return of rental income yourself or are you going to employ someone to do this on your behalf?

Benefits from investing in residential property

Purchasing a property for investment purposes can be a highly tax efficient and low-risk method of investment for the future. It is an area which has seen a significant growth over the past decade.

There is a number of benefits from investing in residential property. Outlined below are just some of these.

Leveraging one's investment

If you purchase a property for €210,000 and borrow 90%, you put down the 10% from your own resources, plus say €12,000 set-up and fit-out costs, the economics are:

Asset Value	€210,000
Contribution	€33,000.
	(€210,000 x 10% + €12,000)

If returns are say 5% p.a. on both property and on an alternative investment, you would expect:

Return on property @ 5% =	€10,500 Gross
	(€210,000 x 5%)
Return on an alternative investment @ 5% =	€1,650 Gross
	(€33,000 x 5%)

Rental income

Regular rental income can cover some or all of the mortgage taken out to buy the property. This is a great attraction in investing in residential property, in that you can earn a rental equal to or greater than your monthly mortgage repayments.

Security
You are investing in a tangible asset in the form of bricks and mortar.

Potential capital appreciation
Property values have increased significantly since 1995 and continue to increase steadily, albeit at a slower rate. Depending on the property and its location, investors could enjoy increases of between 5% and 10% on their asset each year.

Interest rates
Rates are currently at a 50-year historic low. Investors are now able to avail of home-loan interest rates, interest-only mortgages and tracker mortgages.

Mortgage interest relief
The reintroduction of mortgage interest relief means that you can deduct the interest on your mortgage loan from your rental income before it is liable for tax.

Capital allowances
If you purchase items to furnish a property, capital allowances are allowed on these. The costs can be deducted from your rental income for tax purposes. The current allowance is 12.5% of the cost over an eight-year period.

Sectioned property
Section 50 or 23-type properties allow some portion of the capital cost to be deducted from the rental income of all investment properties situated in Ireland.

Allowable deductions against rental income
Rental income arising from a residential investment property in Ireland by an Irish resident is taxed under Schedule D, case five of the income tax code. Certain deductions are allowed against rent to arrive at 'net rent', or in simple terms the taxable amount.

When you purchase a property for investment purposes some expenses incurred by you prior to letting out the property will not in general be allowed as deductions against your rental income.

However once rental income arises and there is a change in tenant, any further expenses incurred in having to get another tenant would not be considered as 'pre-letting' and would typically be regarded as part of the ongoing day-to-day expenses incurred in letting. They would therefore be allowable as a deduction for tax purposes.

Examples of those recurring expenses that are allowable against rental income would include:

- Property insurance
- Repairs carried out on the property
- Legal fees on the second and subsequent lettings, i.e. drawing up a lease agreement
- Accountancy fees for preparing an annual rental income account
- Letting agent and management fees
- Local authority fees, e.g. rates payable by the landlord provided they are required under the lease, such as water rates or refuse collection fees
- Mortgage protection policy premiums

If you were to spend or borrow money for fixtures and fittings a deduction for the expenses incurred would be allowed by way of capital allowances, which are currently 12.5% per annum over an eight-year period. An example of this is if you were to spend €10,000 on 'white goods' to furnish your newly purchased investment property you would get an allowance of €1,250 each year lasting for eight years which can be offset against your rental income.

If you were to spend money to extend the property's size, for example, this would generally not be allowable against your rental income but instead allowed for capital gains calculations if you were to sell the property.

Probably the single biggest deduction allowable against your rental income is the interest you are paying on borrowed moneys used to purchase the property. Since 1998 a number of governments have intervened in some way regarding this measure. At times interest was allowable as a deduction and at other times it was withdrawn but as it stands now, all the interest that is paid to your lender on the mortgage secured on the investment property is fully deductible against your rental income. So for example let's assume your rate of interest is 3.55% and your monthly repayment based upon borrowings of €200,000 is €1,166 over a 20-year period. The interest element of this repayment is €591.67 (€200 x 3.55% = €7,100/12 = €591.67) and it is this amount that is fully allowable against your rental income each month.

Capital gains tax on investment properties

One of the main reasons property is purchased for investment is in the hope the property will appreciate in value over time so that the investor will make a profit on their initial investment. The sale of a property may give rise to a tax on the profit, which is called Capital Gains Tax (CGT). This type of tax was first introduced in April 1974.

Your main private residence on up to one acre is generally exempt from Capital Gains Tax were you to sell it, so the sale of your private home is straightforward from a CGT point of view – there is none.

Capital Gains Tax is charged at a flat rate of 20%. It is calculated by reference to the sale proceeds or market value of the property at the date of the sale. You are allowed to deduct the cost of the asset, i.e. its original purchase price, and other costs such as solicitor's fees, stamp duty paid and enhancement expenditure (substantial capital expenditure incurred in improving the house or apartment – an extension for example) and selling expenses, i.e. auctioneering and solicitor's fees. It has to be remembered that capital expenditure on items such as furniture and kitchen appliances are allowed only against rental income for income-tax purposes and are therefore not allowable to offset for capital gains purposes.

The costs that you are allowed for CGT purposes are 'indexed' in line with inflation when arriving at a taxable gain. This has the effect of increasing the expenditure allowed on the asset in line with the rise in the consumer price index since the asset was bought.

You are allowed an annual capital gains allowance of €1,270 when calculating any potential liability.

Let's look at a basic example:

You purchased a property in 1995 for €100,000. When you bought this you incurred solicitor's costs of €2,000. You sell the property in 2002 for €250,000 and the expenses you incurred were €4,000.

	Cost	Indexed cost	
Sale proceeds less costs	(€250,000–4,000)		€246,000
Purchase Price	€100,000	€151,000	
Incidental costs	€2,000	€3,020	
		€154,020	€154,020
Taxable gain			€91,980
Annual allowance			€1,270
Chargeable gain			€90,710
Capital gains tax @ 20%			€18,142

If you dispose of two properties and make a chargeable gain on the sale of one and a loss on the other you can offset your loss against your gain, so if you made a chargeable gain of €50,000 on Property A and a loss of €20,000 on Property B your overall chargeable gain for the year is €30,000.

It is worth noting that owners of older homes built on large sites who decide to sell off a portion of their site for the purposes of constructing a dwelling may be liable for capital gains tax. Also, if the property or part of it is sold for 'commercial development' (e.g. a supermarket, block of apartments) this in turn may be liable for capital gains tax.

Individuals who are residing in Ireland but have properties in, for example, England or Spain will be subject to CGT on the profits made on the disposal of these properties regardless of where they are situated. In this way the sale of an investment property by an Irish resident in London is subject to Irish CGT. Those who are not resident in Ireland are liable to capital gains tax here only if they dispose of a property or land that is situated in Ireland.

Indexation relief for the purposes of calculating gains on the disposal of a property liable to capital gains tax will not be available for expenditure incurred from the tax year 2003 and subsequent years of assessment, so if you disposed of a property before 1 January 2003 the relief will only have applied from the time you first owned the property up to 31 December 2002.

When does capital gains tax have to be paid?

If you dispose of a property which gives rise to a liability on or before 30 September in a tax year you must pay your capital gains tax by 31 October of the same year.

If you sell the property between 1 October and 31 December of a tax year the liability must be paid before 31 January of the following tax year.

Stamp duty for investment purchases

Threshold	Rate (New and Secondhand)
Up to €127,000	0%
€127,001–190,500	3%
€190,501–254,000	4%
€254,000–317,500	5%
€317,501–381,000	6%
€381,001–635,000	7.5%
Over €635,000	9%

Costs associated with an investment purchase

The amount a lending institution is prepared to advance to you will depend on whether you are a first-time investor or hold multiple investment properties. Typically if you are purchasing an investment property for the first time the maximum amount a lender will advance to you, using the property mortgaged as security alone, will be 90% of the purchase price of the property. So if you are purchasing an investment property costing €250,000 the 10% required from you will be €25,000.

Some lenders are nervous when it comes to first-time investment purchasers. Some lenders will limit the amount they will advance to maybe 85% of the purchase price or less, so you may even have to contribute up to 15% of the cost of the property. They must have a comfort knowing that if the property is unoccupied for a number of months you have the capacity to meet the repayments from your own income. So they will not rely solely on rental income as a means of repaying the amount advanced. They will factor this additional income in but will deduct up to 20% of the projected rental income to allow for unoccupancy. When looking at rental income, some lenders will insist that the rental income you are projected to be in receipt of is at least one and a half times your monthly repayment.

If you have a number of investment properties a lender may be more comfortable with you as they can view your repayment history on other investment borrowings and you can show that you clearly know what you are doing. If sufficient equity has built up on other properties owned by you then they may be prepared to advance up to 100% or more of the new purchase price providing they can have a 'cross charge' on another property so that the sum total of your borrowings on both properties used (new and old) do not exceed more than 85% of the combined value of the properties used as security.

It is worth noting at this point that if you are an experienced investor or have held a buy-to-let mortgage for more than 12 months, some lenders will now assess your ability to borrow based purely on the rental income you are likely to receive from your new purchase. So provided your projected rental income is at least 1.4 times the interest portion of your monthly repayment you would qualify for that amount of mortgage. Your own income is therefore not factored into the equation. An example of this would be that if you were going to receive about €1100 per month in rental income it would allow you a capacity to borrow approximately €250,000:

i.e. €250,000 x 3.7% = €9,250
€9,250 x 1.4 = €12,950
€12,950 ÷ 12 = €1,079

The next thing that you have to factor in is stamp duty and, as can be seen from the table above, the percentage applicable will depend on the purchase price. As an example let's stick to a purchase price of €250,000. Then the stamp duty applicable will be 4% so this will cost you €10,000 i.e. €250,000 x 4% = €10,000.

Legal fees will depend on whether you are using a solicitor charging a fixed flat fee irrespective of the purchase price or a percentage of the purchase price. The difference can be significant, so make sure you know how your solicitor is going to calculate charges.

Indemnity bond fees may apply if you are borrowing more than 85% of the purchase price of your property so ask your potential lender if such a fee is applicable to you and if so how much it is going to be.

A valuation will be required by your lender so a valuation fee of between €130 and €200 may apply.

Finally, you will possibly have to furnish your new investment property. If you purchase a second-hand property it may come with contents included so this is a factor you will not have to consider. But if you are purchasing a new property you will have to allow for the cost of furnishing the property in its entirety. Tenants will expect the contents in the property they are renting to be of good quality so make sure you budget well for this consideration.

So when you are purchasing an investment property your personal outlay is considerable. As can be seen from the above, if a property costs you €250,000 and you are borrowing 90% of the purchase price your 10% contribution and stamp duty alone will account for €35,000, before you furnish your property or pay legal fees.

How to become a landlord for less than €8,000

I am frequently asked by new and existing clients to explore the possibility of arranging finance for them so they can purchase a property with a view to renting it.

The reasoning behind their idea varies. Some will view the property as a long-term investment which will hopefully be a valuable asset in the years ahead and could be used, for example, to supplement their income in retirement. Others want to buy a property now for their children to live in when they go to college. There are also those who have a number of investment properties and may need a 'rental income shelter' and need to buy, for example, a Section 50 or 23 property so they can use the allowances on this type of property to avoid paying tax on the income from other rental properties they have.

Then there are those who have a short-term view of an investment property purchase: they are looking to sell the property after a short period of time, in the hope that it will have increased sufficiently in value since they purchased it to realise a nice profit.

Regardless of the reasons behind the purchase, it is very

important that people know full-well what they are undertaking, especially those who are purchasing for the first time. Factors for people to consider include monthly mortgage repayments, what can and cannot be allowed as deductions against rental income, the obligations they have as landlords, the financial input required by them and the likely rental income.

At present, I believe that the single biggest factor that prevents someone from entering the property market as an investor is the financial contribution they themselves have to make. As already stated, a first-time investment purchaser is likely to have an outlay of €35,000 on a property costing €250,000 before the property is furnished or legal fees paid. This is a lot of money to put forward and people are understandably nervous to commit such a large amount of their savings towards such a venture. If they do not have this amount in savings they may have to remortgage to raise the funds needed and they often wonder if it is worth the hassle.

So is there a solution? Would people be more inclined to purchase a buy-to-let property if their personal contribution was lower? I believe the answer is yes. But can this be done? The answer is: it can.

Your equity requirements when purchasing a new buy-to-let property can be substantially reduced by gaining access to the VAT charged by the developer and by recording the VAT on fit-out, professionals fees and so on.

For example, in the scenario outlined above a 90% mortgage, stamp duty and legal fees on a property costing €250,000 will leave you needing to contribute at least €37,000 towards the purchase. But the tax refund you would receive if you were to register for VAT and claim back the VAT on the purchase would amount to about €29,735, leaving you with a net investment cost of just €7,265 before you furnish the property. And of course, some new investment properties will come fully furnished.

Now let's look at the cost of a 90% mortgage on a purchase price of €250,000, i.e. €225,000. The monthly repayment, assuming a variable rate on an interest-only basis of 3.5%, would come to just €656.25 per month. So in order for your mortgage to be self-financing you would need to achieve this amount in rental income from your property. Is it possible? The question is: if you do find that property, is it more suitable in your present circumstances to become a landlord where the net set-up cost to you could be under €8,000?

In order to claim back the VAT on a property it has to be (a) located in the Irish Republic (b) new and (c) you have to register for VAT before the property you are buying is finished and the sale completed.

The VAT you claim back will obviously have to be repaid in full but it is like getting an 'interest-free-loan' as the amount claimed back and received is the same amount you have to repay in full. You will repay this amount by charging VAT on your rent at 21%, so bear this figure in mind particularly when looking at your monthly mortgage repayment as you will have to deduct this amount from your gross rent.

If you sell the property you will have to repay any VAT outstanding from the sale proceeds.

A final point worth noting is that stamp duty should be payable on the pre-VAT value of the property and not on the purchase price. So rather than paying 4% stamp duty on a new property costing €250,000 – i.e. €10,000 – the stamp is payable on €220,264 – i.e. €8,810 – another cashflow saving of €1,190 to you.

This method is a way of reducing your initial outlay by a considerable amount. It will not suit everyone but it may be an option worth exploring further.

What is a Section 23-type property?

In the early 1980s the government started to introduce tax reliefs for home-owner occupiers and investors who built, refurbished or purchased property in run-down areas. The objective at the time was to encourage the regeneration of these designated areas, raise living standards, reduce crime and generally create a better social fabric in them.

Section 23 reliefs are in the area of capital allowances and income tax. Owner-occupiers of new Section 23 type properties are allowed to offset 5% per annum of the cost against taxable income for a period of ten years while those purchasing a refurbished Section 23 property can offset 10% per annum of the cost against taxable income.

Investors are provided with tax relief on the capital expenditure incurred on the construction, refurbishment or conversion of rented residential accommodation. They are allowed to offset their rental income on all the Irish properties they own against the qualifying allowances, regardless of whether or not the properties are in designated areas.

So how does it work for an owner-occupier? Well, first of all in order to qualify, the property must be occupied by the individual as his or her sole or main residence and they must be the first owner and first occupier of the property after the expenditure has been incurred. Secondly the relief is calculated by reference to the price paid to the developer minus the site cost which does not qualify. The developer will usually determine a percentage (normally between 80% and 95%) of the costs incurred by him which relate to the construction. This percentage is the qualifying amount of the purchase price.

For example, if a newly constructed apartment cost €200,000 with a qualifying cost of 90% the following would apply:

Cost of apartment	€200,000
Qualifying expenditure at 90%	€180,000
Owner occupier relief @ 5% per annum €9,000 (€180,000 x 5%)	
Owner occupier relief over ten years	€90,000
Marginal tax rate	42%
Owner occupier tax credit per annum €3,780 (€9,000 x 42%)	
Total owner occupier relief over ten years	€37,800
Real cost of apartment	€162,200 (€200,000–€37,800)

So in this case the owner-occupier purchaser can reduce their taxable income by 5% per annum, which is €3,780 per year or €315 per month. This amount could significantly reduce their mortgage repayments so that the net monthly cost of borrowings of €184,000 could be as low as €295.

As stated previously in order to qualify for this relief the property must be used as your main residence and it must comply with Section 23 floor-area limits and qualify for a certificate of reasonable cost. No clawback of provisions will apply in the case of owner-occupier relief where the property is sold. However only the first purchaser is entitled to the relief and no transfer of allowances is allowed on the subsequent sale.

If the qualifying expenditure in the above example were the same investors would have an allowance of €180,000 which can be used to offset against all other Irish rental income. This would mean that if a landlord had sufficient other Irish rental income they could potentially save €79,200 in tax (assuming the landlord pays income tax at he marginal rate of 42% plus 2% levies) again reducing the real cost of an apartment costing €200,000 to €120,800 before stamp duty. Any unused relief can be carried forward against any Irish rental income until the allowances have been used in full.

Section 23 owner-occupier and related reliefs are to end in December 2006. If, however, an existing project has incurred at least 15% of its construction costs by the end of December 2006 and meets the scheme conditions the purchaser can avail of:

- 75% of relief on qualifying expenditure from 1 January 2007 to 31 December 2007
- 50% of relief from 1 January 2008 to 31 July 2008. No further relief is available thereafter.

What is a Section 50 property?

Section 50 relief is similar to Section 23 relief: investors who purchase a property whose purpose will be residential accommodation for third-level students are entitled to deduct the qualifying cost of the construction, conversion or refurbishment of the property against any other Irish-based rental income.

So if a property cost €210,000 and the percentage qualifying for allowances was 90%, i.e. € 189,000, this amount could be used as a deduction against all Irish-based rental income.

Let me give you a basic example of how this would work:

Rental income statement 2004

Annual net rental income (property A)	€10,000
Tax payable @44% (42% tax rate plus levies)	€4,400

So this investor is paying tax of €4,400 on his rental income from property A. He purchases a new Section 50 property for €210,000 with 90% allowances i.e. €189,000.

Rental income statement 2005

Annual net rental income (property A)	€10,000
Annual net rental income (property B – S.50)	€8,000

Total net annual income   €18,000
Capital allowances from Section 50 property   €18,000-
Tax payable   €0
The capital allowances used in 2005 were €18,000 and the allowances carried forward for future rental income will be €171,000 (€189,000–€18,000)

The Section 50 relief is available as a deduction against other Irish-based rental income from year one provided the property is fully let under a qualifying lease agreement.

The Section 50 tax break is for a 10-year period and once this term expires, owners are free from their Section 50 obligations and can use the unit in whatever way they see fit. However, if the allowable deductions are not used within the 10-year period, they can be carried forward until such time as they are used in full.

A clawback of the allowances you claim will arise if the property is sold within a period of 10 years. The owner is treated as if they had received additional taxable income, equal to the value of the allowances already claimed in the tax year the property was sold. If a clawback arises, under current legislation the subsequent purchaser can claim the full allowances over the remaining term of the 10 years.

In order to qualify for Section 50-type relief, the accommodation/development must be within an eight-kilometre radius of a relevant campus and must be approved by the college. In addition, the property must conform to certain guidelines issued by the Minister for Education with regard to the accommodation's design and standard.

This type of scheme was introduced to increase the availability of rental accommodation for students and relieve the pressure on the private sector in providing such accommodation.

Pension mortgages

A pension mortgage is an interest-only type mortgage combined with a personal or occupational-type pension plan. The concept is quite simple: an interest-only loan is taken out, combined with regular repayments into your pension plan. At retirement the borrower is expected to repay the mortgage outstanding in full from the lump-sum retirement benefit available under their pension agreement.

The attractions of a pension mortgage are primarily the tax benefits available in funding a pension. The contributions paid into a pension plan are tax deductible within certain limits at your marginal rate of tax. So, for example, if you are paying tax at 42% and your pension premiums are €400 per month you will get tax relief of €168 per month i.e. €400 x 42% so the real cost to you on a monthly basis will be just €232.

As your pension premiums are being used as a vehicle to repay the capital amount borrowed, it effectively means tax deductible capital repayments. This is in contrast to a capital and interest type repayment method where no relief is available at all on capital repayments.

The second benefit is that you will get tax-free growth within your pension fund. Contributions to a pension are invested in tax-exempt funds. This allows contributions to your pension fund to grow at a faster pace than, for example, savings in a deposit account where tax is payable on any interest earned.

Finally the most important factor, especially when considering a pension mortgage option, is that you are entitled to a tax-free lump sum on your accumulated fund at retirement. It is this tax-free lump sum that many will aim to use to repay the amount outstanding on their mortgage.

The lump-sum retirement benefits can arise from three different types of pension arrangements:

- A personal pension plan or PRSA
- An occupational pension scheme
- Additional voluntary contributions (AVCs)

A personal pension plan or PRSA can be taken out by either by a self-employed person with an income arising from a trade or profession or a PAYE employee in non-pensionable employment.

With this type of pension plan you can retire at any time between the ages of 60 and 75, or earlier because of a serious illness or depending on your occupation. When you retire you can take up to 25% of the accumulated fund as a tax-free lump sum with the balance used to:

- Buy an annuity-type pension
- Invest in an approved retirement fund
- Take the balance as a cash sum liable to income tax

It is important to note that in order to avail of the approved retirement fund or take the balance as a taxable lump sum liable to income tax you first have either to invest €63,500 in an approved minimum retirement fund (AMRF) or show you have an income for life that exceeds €12,700 per annum.

So if you borrowed money on an interest-only basis and you were using your pension fund at retirement to repay in full the amount outstanding it could be repaid from either:

- The tax-free lump sum only, if sufficient or combined with
- The after-tax lump sum

Let's look at some examples of repaying the mortgage from the above:

Tax free lump sum only

Patrick is getting a mortgage in the amount of €250,000. If he decides to repay the mortgage from the tax-free lump sum only from his personal pension plan or PRSA he would need to accumulate a fund at retirement of at least €1,000,000 i.e. 25% of €1,000,000 is €250,000.

If he decides to repay the amount outstanding using the tax-free element and the balance as taxable cash the accumulated fund that Patrick will require at retirement will depend on two factors:

a) how much if anything he is required to invest in an approved minimum retirement fund (minimum amount of €63,500 if he does not have a guaranteed income for life of at least €12,700); b) the effective rate of tax he will have to pay on the taxable lump sum.

After-tax lump sum plus requirement to invest €63,500 in an AMRF

If Patrick does have to contribute €63,500 to an AMRF and we are assuming his average tax rate will be calculated at 30% (part at the standard rate and part at the marginal rate) on any taxable lump-sum benefit he takes, taking into account rate bands and tax credits: based on this and allowing for his 25% tax-free lump sum, he would need to accumulate a total retirement fund of at least €380,000 at the age of 60.

€380,000 x 25% tax free element =	€95,000
Needs to invest in AMRF =	€63,500
Taxable lump sum is therefore	€221,500
	(€380,000–€158,500)
Less tax at say 30% =	€155,050
	(€221,500 x 30% = €66,450)
Total tax lump sum is	€95,000 + €155,050 = €250,050

After-tax lump sum with no requirement to invest 63,500 in an AMRF

If he did not have to invest €63,500 in an approved minimum retirement fund and assuming the same tax rate Patrick would need to accumulate a retirement fund of €323,000

€323,000 x 25% tax free element =	€80,750
Needs to invest in AMRF =	€0
Taxable lump sum is therefore	€242,250
	(€323,000 – €80,750)
Less tax at say 30% =	€169,575
	(€242,250 x 30% = €72,675)
Total tax lump sum is	€80,750 + €169,575 = €250,325

If you were to repay the loan from the tax-free lump sum element only you would have to build a retirement fund that is four times the size of your loan, so depending on your age and net relevant earnings the premiums required to build that lump sum could be considerable. Not all of these may qualify for tax relief.

Your premiums will qualify for tax relief depending upon your age:

Age	% of earnings eligible for tax relief
Under 30	15%
30–39	20%
40–49	25%
Over 50	30%

If you are using a taxable lump sum together with the tax-free lump sum and have to invest €63,500 in a minimum approved retirement fund you would have to build a fund that is at least 1.5 times your loan amount, reducing to just 1.3 times if there is no repayment to an AMRF required .

Gross monthly premiums based on the above examples will vary from approximately €1,480 should you require a fund using just the tax-free lump sum to €480 should you use the tax-free lump sum and the balance as a taxable lump sum with no requirement for an AMRF. This is a significant difference in monthly premiums, you will agree. These figures are based on a male aged 36 next birthday, retiring at age 60, assuming a salary of €60,000.

Occupational pension scheme

Under an occupational-type pension arrangement the lump sum that can be taken by an employee at retirement is based upon their number of years of service and their total final salary at retirement date.

Typically an employee will be provided with a lump sum of 3/80ths of their final salary for each completed year's service up to a maximum of 120/80ths. So an employee could get 150% of their final salary as a tax-free lump sum provided they have completed at least 20 years' service.

An example of this is where someone is at retirement age and has a total final salary of €60,000 and has completed 25 years with their company. The maximum lump-sum entitlement that could therefore be provided to them would be €90,000 (€60,000 x 150%)

If we were to use the same example as we did with the personal pension or PRSA route and were borrowing €250,000, our final salary would need to be €166,667 to repay the amount owing in full from our tax-free lump sum. We do not have the comfort under an occupational pension plan of using the balance of the accumulated fund as a taxable lump sum as we have to buy an annuity-type pension with the remainder of our fund. This leads me nicely on to Additional Voluntary Contributions.

Additional Voluntary Contributions

If you think that on retirement the benefits accumulated under an occupational-type pension scheme will be insufficient, you can make what are called Additional Voluntary Contributions (AVCs).

This is an arrangement whereby employees who are members of their company's occupational pension scheme can top up their retirement benefits at their own expense. Those who do contribute

AVCs can normally take the greater part of their AVC fund on retirement as a tax-free lump sum so if needs be they can top up their tax-free lump sum to the maximum allowable.

An example of this is if someone was about to retire after 22 years of service and their total final salary was €60,000. They contributed to an AVC fund which has accumulated a fund of €50,000 at retirement.

The employer has promised to pay a lump sum in relation to the number of years completed service by the employee which would be 22 x 3/80ths of the final salary of €60,000, so this lump sum would amount to €49,500. However the maximum lump sum allowable which can be provided in total between the scheme benefits and the AVCs amounts to 150% x €60,000 = €90,000.

So the employee can use €40,500 of their AVC fund to top up their lump-sum retirement benefit to the maximum allowed, which is €90,000.

The balance of their AVC fund – €9,500 – can be used to secure a pension along with the scheme rules or it can also be taken as a taxable lump sum or invested in an approved retirement fund.

In the Finance Act of 2002 AVC contribution limits were increased to bring them into line with limits applying to a personal pension plans, as outlined previously.

Director's pension mortgages

It is worth noting that directors of a company who control at least 5% of the voting rights within a three-year period prior to retirement can avail of either the benefits arising from a personal pension route or from an occupational-type scheme. This type of pension mortgage is usually arranged by means of the director borrowing the funds personally, whilst the company contributes to a pension fund owned by the director so as to provide sufficient benefits on retirement to repay in full the director's loan. The director's only personal contribution is towards the interest repayment to the lender on the borrowed moneys.

A director's pension mortgage has a number of advantages for those who wish to use a pension mortgage to repay an amount borrowed:

- You can target a fund that is equal to the tax-free lump sum only, so it is not necessary to accumulate a fund up to four times the loan amount.
- There is no benefit-in-kind liablity to the director on contributions made by the company to their pension plan.
- The cost of the pension premiums can be paid in total by the company so there is no personal cost to the director.
- The only personal outlay by the director would be the interest repayments to the bank, which might be deductible against, for example, rental income.

As you can see from the above it may be very beneficial for a director of a company who controls at least 5% of the voting rights to use a pension mortgage to repay the amount borrowed.

Things to bear in mind

Whilst funding the eventual repayment of a loan by way of a pension mortgage can be a very tax-efficient way of structuring your finances, a note of caution has to be borne in mind:

Because the earliest age you are allowed to take your pension from is 60 you would typically have to be of a certain age before a pension mortgage route would be allowable by a lender. For example if you were 30 and mortgaged a property with a 25-year term you could not access your pension fund for another five years, How would you repay the amount outstanding without having to sell the property?

Secondly, depending on how much you borrow, you may need to make significant contributions to your pension to build up the required fund to repay the amount outstanding. Can you afford these premiums?

Should you use the entire pension fund to repay the amount owing, you are of course eliminating your entire fund for future income apart from what is invested in an AMRF. So make sure you have alternative provisions in place to provide an income after your retirement.

If the reason you chose the pension mortgage route in the first place was to fund the repayment in full of an investment property purchased by you then maybe the rental income from this property would be a great source of income in retirement for you.

The final factor that also needs to be borne in mind is that a pension mortgage involves an element of risk: that the pension plan you are funding into will not produce enough of a return to repay the full mortgage outstanding.

7
Insurances

Life assurance

It is a legal requirement that all home loans should have life cover. This is to protect (a) the lender who will have the loan amount outstanding to them repaid in full from the proceeds of the borrower's life policy and (b) to protect the borrowers in the event of one passing away so that the surviving party is not left having to continue repaying the monthly mortgage. Indeed it will also protect the beneficiary of a property left by a single person.

Life cover must be for the amount and term of your mortgage loan.

If, for example, there is a joint mortgage, the death occurs of the main breadwinner and there is no life policy in place to repay the outstanding mortgage, it may be an unrealistic option for the surviving party to sell the property and repay the mortgage from the proceeds, especially if the deceased leaves a spouse and dependants.

If such an unfortunate event were to happen, it may increase the risk of the mortgage going into arrears and the survivor ultimately defaulting with the loan repayments. This could lead to the repossession of the property, which is something neither the lender nor the borrower wants to happen.

There is a number of different life assurance policies you can effect and I will outline some to you below.

Decreasing life cover

This is also referred to as a mortgage protection policy and is a decreasing form of life assurance. If you elect to repay your mortgage by an interest and capital-type arrangement you know that part of your monthly repayment is going towards reducing some part of the original sum borrowed. You continue to make repayments until the mortgage has run its course and you no longer owe any money to your lender.

If you effect a mortgage protection policy to repay your mortgage, on death the life cover on it will reduce in line with the loan amount outstanding, thereby clearing the amount that is outstanding on your mortgage at the date of death. Arrears are, however, excluded.

The premiums for such a policy are fixed from the outset and although the life cover will reduce over time, the premiums will not. At the end of the term nothing is payable and there is no surrender value. Due to the fact that the amount of cover reduces over time it is usually the cheapest form of cover.

Term assurance

This form of life cover insures you for the same amount throughout the agreed term. So, for example, if you effected such a policy for €200,000, the same amount as your mortgage, and you were to die years later when there is just €100,000 outstanding, a sum of €200,000 would be paid from the life company. This amount would first clear your mortgage of €100,000 with the remaining €100,000 being paid to your estate or to the surviving member on the policy schedule, if there is one.

If your method of mortgage repayment is by interest only this is the type of policy you will have to take out because you would not be reducing anything off your mortgage and a lender would insist on your having sufficient cover in place to repay their mortgage in full in the event of death. This type of policy is normally more expensive than decreasing mortgage protection cover but again, at the end of the term, nothing is payable and there is no surrender value.

Serious illness cover

Most people do not realise that one out of every four men and one in five women will be diagnosed with a serious illness before they reach retirement age. These will include cancer, stroke or heart attack and a range of serious or chronic illnesses.

So if you or those who depend on you would face financial hardship if you were diagnosed with a serious illness, it may be worth considering adding serious illness to either of the policies described above. If you become seriously ill the last thing you want is any financial worry such as the fear of losing your home because you cannot repay the mortgage. Having serious illness cover will give you peace of mind in these circumstances.

Convertible option

If you decide to include this option with your life policy it will mean that you can convert to another policy without giving further evidence of your state of health.

If you have a young family and are on a tight budget having this option may be a good idea. It will give you valuable options in later years if your income rises or your health declines.

How much will it cost?

The premiums for the above policies are normally based upon factors such as:

- The sum assured
- Age
- Term of policy
- Smoker status
- Current health status

The premiums can vary from one insurance company to another.

Let's look at an example of a single male, aged 32 and a non-smoker borrowing a sum of €220,000 over a 35-year period.

At the moment the cheapest monthly premium for a mortgage-protection policy for this individual is €19.32 for a decreasing policy and €27.97 for a level-term assurance policy. If you include serious-illness cover in the amount of €40,000 (we will take this figure as we will assume his salary is this amount) the premium will increase to €28.90 on a decreasing basis and €48.01 on a term-assurance basis.

If this individual is a smoker his premium is likely to rise by between €10 and €20 per month depending on the life policy taken out. If he is to include serious illness his premium will increase by an extra €30 per month. Now there is an incentive to kick the habit!

When life cover is not required for mortgage purposes

There are some cases when life cover will not be required as additional security for the mortgage you have taken out:

- If the property you are purchasing is not your principal private residence
- If you are over the age of 50
- If you have been refused life cover by a life-assurance company
- If you have been accepted for cover but have been 'rated' by a life company with the premiums increasing significantly from what you would have been paid had you been accepted at ordinary rates

However, even though, for example, you are buying a property for investment reasons and will obviously not reside in it, a lender may still insist that you have to take out life cover before they issue your loan cheque. Another example may be if there is a guarantor joining in on a mortgage for their son or daughter for the purpose of securing the amount required. Again the guarantor may not reside in the property and may be over 50 but the lender may still insist that the guarantor have some level of life cover assigned to the loan.

It is therefore decided very much a case-by-case basis and will depend on whether the lender is more comfortable advancing funds to you if there is some level of cover in place.

If a borrower falls into one of the four categories outlined above, they will have to sign a 'life waiver' form. This is required by the lender to confirm that the borrower is not proceeding with life cover for one of the four reasons. If there are two borrowers the other party to the mortgage will have to co-sign the life waiver form to acknowledge that they are aware that their joint borrower has no life cover attaching to the loan.

It can be all too easy to sign a waiver form if you are buying an investment property, for example, but you must be aware of the consequences of your actions. Do you want to leave a property on your death where the beneficiary is liable for the mortgage repayments? Do you know that your monthly repayments for life assurance are deductible against your rental income?

If you have a choice whether to take out life cover or not you must weigh up the advantages and disadvantages before making your decision. One of the advantages of doing so would be having your loan repaid in full on your death and an obvious disadvantage would be where the premiums are very expensive – so take your time before making your decision.

Mortgage payments protection

Mortgage payments protection, or home owner's payment protection, is a mortgage insurance policy whose aim is to cover your mortgage repayments in the event of one of the following:

● Redundancy
● The borrower becoming ill and being unable to work for
  more than a specified period, normally one month

The policy should cover your monthly interest and capital repayments to your lender for a limited period, normally a maximum of twelve months. As with any insurance policy you pay a monthly premium and if the worst happens the policy will start to pay out after the excess period.

Obviously if you are self-employed, redundancy cover will not apply as you cannot make yourself redundant. However if you are self-employed a hospitalisation benefit will apply; this usually takes effect after you have spent ten days in hospital.

If you have ever been out of work due to an illness or were made redundant you will know full well how fast a full salary entitlement or redundancy payment runs out. Mortgage payments protection is designed to bridge this gap so you can concentrate on getting well or getting that new job. It will give you great peace of mind to know that your mortgage repayments are being protected, at least for 12 months.

The cost of your monthly premium will depend on the percentage of your mortgage you want protected. The premium is based on a rate for every €100 of your mortgage repayment you wish to have covered. This cost is normally about €5.00 for every hundred you want covered.

Let's assume your monthly mortgage is €800. If you wanted cover for the full amount it would cost you €40 per month i.e. 8 x €5. The cover is usually sold in blocks of €50. Some lenders may advise you take out the maximum cover possible which is about 120% of your mortgage repayment so as to allow the excess to continue to pay your life-cover premiums and home insurance premiums.

Should a benefit become payable the payment is made directly to the beneficiary's mortgage account.

Where the payments protection is covering two borrowers, the same premium will cover both. However should one person claim, one of the following will apply. Either:

- 50% of the insured benefit will be payable or
- A portion of the benefit will be paid . This will be based on the income of the borrower who is making the claim relative to the combined income of both borrowers.

There are some restrictions when applying for this cover and for full details you should check the terms and conditions. You would be expected have been in full employment for a certain period of time to qualify for benefits under the redundancy section. You should also not expect to be made redundant or have any expectation of unemployment within three months of going on cover. Other restrictions would include: claims arising from pregnancy or childbirth; HIV-related illness; suicide or the wilful self-exposure to danger by the insured borrower; any illness or disability the person applying for cover would have been aware of within one year before going on cover.

Home insurance
As with life assurance, lenders will insist that the property you are purchasing and on which they have advanced you money should be adequately insured against fire, subsidence, flood damage, accidental damage, storm damage and so on.

There is a number of factors that will influence the cost and level of your home insurance, of which just some are:

- The size and rebuilding costs of the property
- The age and type of property

- Any history of storm or flood damage in the area
- The property's current state of repair

When you are searching for a home insurance quotation, you should base your quote on a figure that represents the full rebuilding cost, i.e. the amount it would take to rebuild your house again if it was totally destroyed.

This is also referred to as the reinstatement value of the property. This reinstatement figure will appear on the valuation report that was carried out on your property by your lender's appointed valuer and will also appear on your offer letter.

The location of your property can be a factor in the price and recommended reinstatement value of your home insurance. Unfortunately if you are living in a perceived high risk area, it can affect your premium.

Combined building and contents insurance policies are now a common feature with most insurance companies, whereby contents cover will automatically be based on a percentage of the property's building insurance cover, For example, if the property is insured for €200,000 contents will automatically be covered for 40% of this amount – €80,000.

Your premium for contents insurance can also be influenced by other factors, such as:

- Whether you want all-risks or standard cover
- Whether you have secure locks on your doors and windows
- Whether you have an alarm fitted and if so what type
- Whether the property is unoccupied for long periods of time
- The exact type and value of specified items

Many people today are overinsuring their properties as they feel the current market value of the property is the figure they need to insure it for. This is not the case. An insurance company will pay out only a sum of money that will rebuild the property to its former state and not a sum based on its resale value. However, better overinsured than under, so I suggest that you check what you are actually insured for and if you are unsure whether the sum is too large or too small you should have your property assessed again.

The insurance market is competitive at the moment and when sourcing an insurer for your property you should consult an independent home-insurance broker who will be able to compare quotes from the various insurance providers.

Protect your income!

Have you ever asked yourself what would happen to your income if you were out of work for a long period of time? How long would your current employer pay your salary and how much of your salary would they pay? And if, for example, they paid it for only three months, how much of a benefit would you then be entitled to?

It is amazing the number of people who do not know how much and for how long their employer would pay them if they were out of work for a period of time. They ask the question when it is too late, when they are out of work and realise that their employer will not cover them at all or only for a short period of time and they have not made the necessary provisions to make up the shortfall.

The current maximum disability benefit payable by the state is €165.80 per week (excluding dependent adults and children). This is such a small amount to be in receipt of when mortgage repayments have to be made, as well as food purchased and bills, provisions for children and transport costs paid. Is it possible to survive on this small amount with all these monthly commitments? I doubt it very much.

So what are you going to do about it and what should you do first? First of all ask your employer how much of your salary and for how long they will pay you if you are out of work for a period of time. That is the starting point. When you know this, you are in a position to put in place a form of cover that will replace your lost income.

Permanent health insurance is a policy that provides an income payment if the insured person has 'suffered a loss of earned income due to being unable to follow his or her own occupation, or any other occupation for which he or she is reasonably suited or trained, due to sickness or disability lasting longer than a certain deferred period, and is not following any other occupation'.

It is important to note that you need to suffer a loss of earned income to qualify for payment of the benefit.

PHI cover and serious-illness cover are often confused. The

difference is that PHI cover pays out a regular income to you until such time you are ready to return to work, whereas serious illness cover pays out one lump sum in the event of your contracting a specified serious illness.

In order to ensure that an individual has an incentive to return to work, there are typically two main restrictions on the PHI cover provided, which are (a) that cover may be restricted to 75% of earnings less any social welfare disability benefits and other ongoing income and (b) that there may be an overall monetary restriction on the cover provided.

PHI premiums rates are very sensitive to the individual's occupation. Life companies tend to grade occupations from one to four. Occupations in Class One would tend to get normal rates whereas occupations in class four might have rates twice the level of someone in occupation class one. There are even some occupations that may not be offered PHI cover at all.

PHI premiums are normally tax deductible up to an annual limit of 10% of your income.

You should be aware of this issue and have provisions in place in case you should, for some reason, be out of work for a long period of time. It is extremely important for self-employed people who obviously do not have an employer to pay their income. If they were out of work, what would they do?

8
The Legal Process

The role of your solicitor

The role that your solicitor is going to play for you in looking after the legal side of your purchase is incredibly important, so you need to select a solicitor who is competent, knowledgeable, reasonably priced and someone who are comfortable with.

The amount of time and effort expended on your behalf by your solicitor often goes unrecognised. We hear people saying, 'Sure aren't they getting paid well' and 'I could do what they do'. We do not fully understand what our solicitor does on our behalf and we do not need to know the full ins and outs but we should have some basic idea of what should be happening. This can give us a better idea of whether everything is going smoothly or not and we can also understand and appreciate a little bit more the significance of the solicitor's role. Below are just some of the issues your solicitor will have to deal with on your behalf:

- Examining the title of the property you are purchasing. If, for example, the property is registered with the Registry of Deeds your solicitor's investigation could be very complicated and time-consuming as they may have to examine all documents concerning the property for the past 25 years.
- Examining the contract for sale supplied by the vendor's solicitor
- Examining the mortgage offer from your lender and advising you about the terms and conditions therein
- Issuing of the solicitor's undertaking regarding the title of the

property
- Raising queries on the title of the property, covering aspects such as planning permission, boundaries, easements
- Forwarding the relevant documents to your lender for approval
- Drafting and execution of the family home declaration
- Examining the terms and conditions of a building agreement; noting building plans, payments clause, insurance clause and your builder's warranty for defects
- Conducting searches on the property and examining these to ensure all are in order
- Execution of the deed of transfer and submitting same to the Revenue Commissioners for adjudication
- Registering the title of the property in the Land Registry
- Forwarding a certificate of title to your lender
- Drafting and executing the contract of sale, deed of mortgage and assignment of life policy

The above tasks are just a sample of what your solicitor has to do for you and I am sure I omitted many more essential things. Some of the points mentioned above will mean absolutely nothing to you but a good solicitor will explain their meaning in simple English and, more importantly, why they are required.

Choosing your solicitor

One of the best ways of selecting a solicitor is by way of a recommendation you receive from a relative or a friend who has used a particular firm in the past. Also ask your mortgage adviser or auctioneer if they would recommend any firm. They may or may not but if you do not know where to start looking they could be of some assistance to you, rather than sticking a pin in the solicitor section of the *Golden Pages*.

It is prudent to have at least two or three firms to choose from. The single biggest factor when people choose a solicitor is the cost. This is a very valid question as prices can vary significantly from those charging a percentage of the purchase price to those charging a flat fee irrespective of price. An example of this is where the purchase price of your property is €200,000. One firm may charge a set fee of €950 plus VAT and outlay and a competing firm charge 1% of the purchase price – €2,000 plus VAT and outlay. As demonstrated by this simple example the savings that you can achieve can be enormous.

However, whilst price is a major factor also consider the following before choosing:

Reputation

Do you know the reputation of the firm you are considering? Has a friend used them in the past and if so how did they feel about the quality of their service?

Specialists

Does the firm have a specialist dedicated conveyancing team? Has the solicitor acting for you got experience in conveyancing? You do not want to choose a solicitor who is slow, inefficient or inexperienced in conveyancing matters or who may not check documents carefully enough because this could give rise to problems in the future.

You want your solicitor to explain things in a way that is easy to understand, return your phone calls if you need to get hold of them; you want someone who knows what they are doing and finally a person you are comfortable dealing with.

People often leave the selection of a solicitor as the very last thing to decide when purchasing a property. They look for properties, compare rates and arrange a mortgage but often leave the solicitor to the last minute. This is particularly the case for first-time buyers. How many times has it happened that deposits are placed on new or second-hand properties and when buyers are asked who their solicitor is, they can't give an answer?

Whether you are a first-time buyer, trading up or an investor, look at who you are going to use as your legal representative as early as possible. It is such an important decision to make that you are better off not having to make it in a hurry.

The legal process in buying your home

Stage 1 – Sale agreed
Seller's solicitor

- They will apply to your present lender for the return of the title documents to the property you are going to sell. In order for them to do this they will first have to get a letter of authority signed by you authorising them to get the title documents back from your lender.
- If the seller has no mortgage they will just bring the title documents in to their solicitor.
- Upon receiving the title documents, the solicitor will prepare a contract for sale which sets out amongst other things the purchase price and what land and buildings the property includes. This will be forwarded to the buyer's solicitor for examination.

Buyer's solicitor

- On receipt of the contracts your solicitor will examine the content of the contract and supporting documentation provided by the seller's solicitor. They will also examine the title to the property their client is buying. They will confirm the sale price, what deposit is required and the completion date.
- Your solicitor may then send you a 'letter of advices' requesting you to check that the details in the contract, such as price, the specifications of the property and any allowances you may be in receipt of are correct.
- Your solicitor will probably forward to you at this stage, if they have not already done so following your initial meeting with them, an estimate as to what their fees are likely to be together with the cost of the legal outlay associated with your purchase i.e. Land Registry fees, registration of your mortgage and stamp duty.
- When you check the documentation your solicitor has forwarded to you and you are happy with it, you should arrange to meet your solicitor to sign the contract and pay your deposit (normally 10% of the purchase price inclusive of

the booking deposit paid to the auctioneer).

- You must have your formal letter of offer from your chosen lender in place before you sign contracts. Your solicitor should also be in receipt of a legal pack from your lender, so that when you are visiting to sign contracts you can discuss, at the same visit, the content of your loan offer and sign the relevant mortgage documentation such as the loan acceptance and assignment of life policy.

- It is not enough to have verbal approval from your lender saying they will grant you the mortgage.

- It is also important before you sign contracts, particularly if you are buying a second-hand property, that you get a structural survey carried out on the property your are buying to ensure that no major structural defects are present. The survey should also highlight other possible areas of the house that may need attention in the future.

Stage 2 – Exchange of contracts

This is an extremely important moment. Up until now both parties could withdraw from the sale/purchase without penalty. Once contracts are signed by both parties and exchanged the agreement becomes legally binding. From this moment on the seller must sell and the buyer must buy and the agreement must be carried out at the purchase price stated in the contract.

Seller's solicitor

- Receives the contracts back from the purchaser's solicitor together with deposit.

- Receives and approves the transfer deed and gets the seller to sign it. This is a document prepared by the buyer's solicitor confirming the transfer of ownership from the seller to buyer.

- The solicitor will have requested a settlement figure from the seller's mortgage company confirming the amount required to redeem their mortgage in full. Their solicitor will also request outstanding balances due on any other loans that their client wishes to pay in full from the proceeds of their sale.

Buyer's solicitor

- They will forward the signed contract together with deposit to the seller's solicitor.
- When the solicitor receives the signed contract back from the seller's solicitor they will send approximately 50 questions in relation to the title of the property to the seller's solicitor which must be answered to the satisfaction of your solicitor and returned.
- Once the questions relating to the title are received back and are in order your solicitor will return the signed contract to the seller's solicitor and then prepare the deed of transfer and the mortgage deed. The mortgage deed is the legal charge on the property to your mortgage lender until such time as the loan is repaid in full.
- The deed of transfer may be sent to the seller's solicitor along with the contract and when it is signed by both the seller and buyer it will be forwarded to the Revenue for stamping on closing. Even if no stamp duty is payable it still must be sent. The deed of transfer will be sent to the Land Registry or Registry of Deeds which record the names of all property owners in Ireland.
- Your solicitor will also get you to sign a Family Home Declaration which needs to be signed by you for the benefit of your mortgage lender. This document has got to be completed for every property purchase. It will confirm things such as whether the property is a family home, the marital status of the purchasers and whether a third party has an interest in the property.
- Your solicitor will notify and prepare your lender by way of a document called a 'cheque requisition form' that they will require funds on a particular date, i.e. the agreed closing date. Please note that the cheque will be provided only when all conditions as outlined in the offer letter are met to the satisfaction of your lender.

Stage 3 – Completion
Seller's solicitor

- Receives the balance of the purchase price from the buyer's solicitor.
- Pays off what is outstanding on the seller's mortgage (if applicable) and any other loans the seller may wish to have repaid in full.
- In return for the balance of moneys owed the seller's solicitor will either give the keys of the property directly to the buyer's solicitor or have them released by the selling agent to the purchasers.
- The solicitor will forward you the balance from the proceeds of the sale or hold part of the funds towards the purchase of a new property if any.

Buyer's solicitor

- When the solicitor receives the loan cheque from your lender they will as standard practice carry out closing searches with for example, the Land Registry, Companies' Office, Sheriff's Office and Bankruptcy Office. The searches will show whether there is an existing mortgage on the property; if any other person has a legal entitlement or interest in the property; that there are no bankruptcy or judgement orders registered against the seller; and that the builder you are buying from has not gone into liquidation.
- Your solicitor will now go to the seller's solicitor's office to arrange completion of the purchase. In exchange for the moneys owed your solicitor will receive the keys to the property and the appropriate documentation with regard to the title of the property.
- You must call to your solicitor's office to sign the appropriate documentation which transfers the title of the property into your name, ensuring you are now the legal owner of the property just purchased.
- Your solicitor will forward documentation including the deed of transfer to the Revenue Commissioners and pay the stamp duty due, if applicable.
- When the documentation is returned to your solicitor by the

Revenue they will send the title documents to the relevant land agency and apply for the registration of your name as the registered owner. They will also have the mortgage secured by you registered on the title of the property (mortgage deed). It can take anything from three months to two years to complete the registration. Once it is complete the Land Registry will notify your solicitor.

Glossary of legal terms

Completion date

This is the date agreed by both parties when the seller will vacate the property and the ownership of the property will pass from seller to buyer.

If this agreed date is not going to be met by either the seller or purchaser due to an unforeseen event this should be communicated as early as possible to the other party so alternative arrangements can be made. For example, it would obviously affect the purchaser if they had given notice in their rented accommodation or it would affect the seller if the purchaser's loan cheque did not arrive on time and they needed these funds to complete the purchase of another property.

Contract

This is the legal document that confirms the sale/purchase of the property. It will confirm what has been agreed, such as the property address, purchase price and the names of the seller/buyer. The contract is drawn up by the seller's solicitor and forwarded to the purchaser's solicitor. Once all queries are answered and both parties are ready to commit legally, the contracts are exchanged.

Conveyancing

This is the legal description for the work involved in transferring the ownership of a property from one person to another.

Deposit

This is the amount paid by the buyer when contracts are exchanged. The amount of the deposit is normally 10% of the purchase price and is inclusive of any deposit paid to the selling agent. The deposit is a part-payment and a form of guarantee by the buyer that they will complete the purchase. If the buyer refuses to complete after having signed contracts, the deposit is forfeited and kept by the seller.

Deeds/title deeds

These are the legal documents that contain information about the property. They will show, among other things, that the person selling the property actually owns the property.

Deed of transfer

Document signed by both parties confirming the transfer of ownership from seller to buyer.

Easement

This is a term referring to the right a property owner may have over adjoining property or land. It could mean they have a right of way or access or a right to a water supply or drainage.

Freehold

This is a legal term for the way an owner holds the property. With freehold the owner owns the property and the land the property is situated on.

Leasehold

This means that you own the property but not the land it stands on. When a lease expires the ownership of the property reverts back to the freehold owner.

Land Registry

This is a central body that retains records of who owns the land and under what conditions.

Mortgage deed

This is a document signed by the borrower agreeing to the terms set out in their mortgage offer. Your lender will have a legal charge on the property until the loan is repaid in full. The document is sent to the Land Registry, which registers the charge on the title of the property.

Mortgage offer

This is a formal written offer by a lending institution to advance a sum of money to you to allow you to purchase a property. The offer will detail the amount of the loan and the repayment period and will also set out the terms and conditions that have to be adhered to.

Redemption figure

The amount of money required to repay a mortgage in full.

Stamp duty

This is a tax payable on the purchase of a property.

Structural survey

This a comprehensive report carried out by a qualified surveyor on the physical state of the property you are buying. It will highlight any defects or areas that may need attention now or in the future and it is strongly recommended that you get one carried out, especially if you are buying a second-hand property.

Searches

These are carried out by the buyer's solicitor to ensure there is nothing that might affect the title of the property you are buying.

9
Manage Your Mortgage

Be smart, plan and budget carefully!
Purchasing a property for either the first or second time will have you concentrating on acquiring your deposit, arranging your mortgage and selling your existing property. With so much to consider and worry about you are relieved when your loan cheque issues and you move into your new property.

Reality will sink in though – and quite quickly at that – as you now have a number of financial responsibilities that come with owning your own property.

You may not have had these responsibilities if you had been living at home or in rented accommodation but you certainly do now. So be smart and plan your expenditure carefully, budget for those fixed monthly outgoings, put money aside for those rainy days – for there will come a time when you will need to call upon these savings.

This is stating the obvious, but avoid going into arrears on your mortgage as your home is a major investment and you have a great deal to lose if you default on your mortgage repayments.

Apart from your mortgage repayments, electricity bill, telephone bill and insurance premiums there will be other expenses you will incur and they can come at the worst possible times. For example your car has a mechanical failure and needs fixing; and plumbing and heating systems in your home need to be fixed or upgraded. This has particular relevance for those who purchase second-hand properties in need of repair. It is all too easy to borrow money from your credit union or bank to pay for these repairs but careful planning, whereby you accumulate a 'reserve fund' through regular savings to cater for these unforeseen events will stand you in great stead for the future.

This reserve fund can be a great source of comfort to you – knowing that if something needs fixing, repairing or improving or more importantly if you were made redundant or suffered a loss in income through an illness or for whatever reason you can at least call on the money in this fund to help you. Everyone should aim to have a reserve fund of at least three times the net monthly household income. Remember this fund is not a Christmas club or holiday fund; it is there to be used in *emergencies*.

Before your house purchase you should have planned carefully and budgeted for the expenses you were going to encounter, such as legal fees, deposit and stamp duty. You should now similarly budget and plan what your fixed outgoings will be so you will know exactly what is going to be debited or withdrawn from your account each month to meet your obligations.

Careful planning and simply knowing what needs to be in your account on a particular day of the month will mean you will have nothing to worry about and if you do at least you can call upon those savings when the unforeseen happens.

Behind with mortgage repayments – what to do!

If you miss one, two or more mortgage repayments with your lender, arrears will obviously build up on your mortgage account.

You could be liable to interest penalties as a result of being in arrears as you are not honouring your commitment to the mortgage agreement. Depending on your lender, this arrears charge will be added to your account each month and can accumulate to such an extent that the penalties alone are significant in size.

Nobody wants to go into arrears and nobody sets out this way. Arrears on mortgages happen for a variety of reasons, ranging from bad management of your finances each month to being made redundant or being unable to work for a period of time due to an accident or a serious illness.

Lending institutions are very conscious of mortgages that go into arrears. Some will have a dedicated team whose job it is to monitor and identify loans which they feel need attention, to avoid the risk of borrowers eventually defaulting altogether on the loan repayments.

So if you are finding it difficult to make your mortgage repayments, for whatever reason, the first thing you should do is to contact your mortgage lender and advise them of your current predicament and circumstances.

A lender will welcome the fact that you are bringing this problem to their attention and will endeavour to work with you to help overcome your current difficulty both in the short and long term. Their last resort will be to seek a court order to repossess your property, so if you talk to your lender, work with them and honour the solution you agree to you will be fine.

On a personal level you have to deal with this issue from the word go. Do not ignore the problem and if you feel you cannot deal with the problem yourself talk to someone who can maybe act as a third party for you, speak to the lender and negotiate on your behalf. Failing to address the situation will make matters a whole lot worse for you in the long run.

To reduce the repayment burden on you some lenders may be prepared to offer you a moratorium on your mortgage repayments. This is where you do not make a full monthly repayment but do agree to the repayment of a notional amount. This amount can vary from lender to lender and can range from €1 to €100 per month. You will, however, have to continue with the full repayment of your life and home insurance premiums. The moratorium may last for a limited period of time and the missed repayments or the difference between what you are repaying and what you should have been repaying are added to the amount you currently owe.

Another solution a lender may suggest is extending the term of your mortgage. Would the extension of, say, ten years to your mortgage reduce your monthly repayment to an amount that is more manageable?

If you were once two or three months in arrears on your mortgage account and have been paying the full instalment now without difficulty for some time but you just cannot find that extra sum each month to reduce the arrears by any reasonable amount your lender may suggest 'cleaning the slate' and adding the arrears on to the amount you currently owe. You will then be starting afresh with no arrears and you will feel much better about it going forward. But be aware that by doing this you are in effect capitalising your arrears and increasing the amount you now owe upon which interest is charged. You are going to be repaying those missed months now over a much longer time, maybe 15 or even 20 years. You will also have to increase your life cover by the amount added to your mortgage account. Regardless of these factors it might be the option which best suits your present circumstances.

Your lender could also consent to interest-only repayments whereby you service only the interest portion of your loan. The difference in repayments between an interest method of repayment and a capital method could be significant and could help you overcome your present difficulties.

There are many other solutions that can be explored with your lender but I cannot stress enough the importance of communicating with your lender if you are in arrears or fear that you are going to be. Then you can explore the options that are available to you and reach a solution you are both happy with.

Removing a name from a mortgage

It is becoming more and more common nowadays that requests for the removal of one name from a joint mortgage are made to lending institutions.

The reasons for the request vary but the single biggest contributory factor is a couple who separate or divorce, with one wanting to remain in the property and the other wanting to move on. Whatever the reason behind the request both parties have to agree to it and make a formal request to their lender.

From a lender's viewpoint, before they will agree to sanctioning the request they first and foremost have to be satisfied that the person who wants to remain on the mortgage has an ability in their own right to repay the mortgage. They will make their judgement based upon factors such as your current net monthly income, any other loan commitments you may have, and the stability of your current employment.

They will also consider other factors when making their judgement. These include the current mortgage's repayment history – is it good or bad? – and the value of the property against the mortgage outstanding. Does the person hoping to stay in the property need additional funds to 'buy out' the other person's interest in the property? If yes, how much is required and is there a clear ability to repay this increased amount on the basis of one income? Will the lender be over-exposing themselves on the amount advanced against the current value of the property?

The remaining person in the property may look at renting out a room to supplement the mortgage repayments. Whilst it is worth telling a lender that this will be your intention, they will normally be reluctant to include it as a second source of income as you may change your mind in the future. However, if you fall just short of qualifying with one income a lender may include this room rental income in order to qualify you for the amount needed; this will be judged very much on a case-by-case basis. Where there are more positives – for example low loan-to-value, stable employment, good job and income prospects, a professional qualification, good repayment history – than negatives, they may allow it.

Have no doubt, though, that if the lender feels the repayments cannot be met by the remaining party as the debt-service ratio is greater than what is allowed (your outgoings exceed a certain percentage of your income, normally between 35 and 40% of your net take-home pay) they can refuse to release the other party from their mortgage obligations. Selling the property might then be your only option. Of course you could also switch lenders as lending criteria differ from lender to lender. Whereas your current lender may not be prepared to advance the sum required another lender may, so this might be worth looking into.

If the lender agrees to the request it will be like taking out a whole new mortgage all over again as they will require items such as a letter from your employer confirming income and permanency, up-to-date payslips and bank statements, your P60, loan account statements and a copy of the separation/divorce agreement.

What happens when a person who has a mortgage dies?

Let's look firstly at what would happen if a person on a joint mortgage were to die. The mortgage obligations in this case are quite simple: they would automatically fall to the surviving borrower.

The majority of mortgages now require that both parties to the mortgage have adequate life cover in place so that in the event of either dying the mortgage is repaid in full from the proceeds of the life assurance policy. If this is the case the surviving borrower will not have to worry about the mortgage repayments.

There are of course occasions when a joint borrower may decide not to effect a life policy if, for example, they are over 50, the mortgaged property is not their principal private residence, or premiums are too expensive. So if they were to die the monthly mortgage repayments would be the responsibility of the remaining borrower. It is very important therefore that the other borrower is aware of their responsibility should their co-borrower pass away in a situation where life cover was not effected. It is prudent to have some form of cover in place that will clear in full or at least eliminate a large part of the sum owed in the event of death.

When the lender is advised of the death of a joint borrower on a mortgage and receives confirmation by way of a death certificate they will amend the details on the mortgage account and the mortgage repayments will have to be continued by the other borrower. This is, of course, if no life policy is in place.

If a life policy is in place the lender will receive the proceeds of the life policy (if assigned) from the life assurance company and if sufficient in size discharge the mortgage completely. This is the best thing that can happen: the remaining borrower is not left with repayments they possibly cannot meet on their own, coonsequently being forced to sell the property. So it is incredibly important, especially for joint borrowers where the mortgage is secured on the family home that (a) sufficient cover is taken out in the first place and (b) the premiums due on the life policy are paid on time, as you do not want cover to stop because of non-payment of your monthly premium.

Where the death occurs on a mortgage where there is just one borrower the obligations will fall to the estate of the deceased. If a life policy has been effected and assigned to the lender prior to the mortgage being drawn down by the now deceased the lender is the beneficiary of the policy. They will receive the proceeds from the life company and repay the mortgage outstanding in full.

If a will has been made, executors will have been appointed who will discharge the estate as per the wishes of the deceased after having collected the assets of the deceased and paid off any debts. If there is a life policy in place that had not been assigned as additional security to a lender, the life assurance company may seek a copy of the grant of probate that was issued by the High Court to the executors before they pay out proceeds of a life policy to them.

If someone died without leaving a will the next of kin will apply to the High Court looking for what is called 'letters of administration' which gives them the authority to collect assets, clear debts, including the mortgage outstanding if possible, and distribute any remaining balance to whoever has a claim to the estate of the deceased under the terms of the 1965 Succession Act. Again, before a life company will pay out the proceeds of an unassigned life policy they may seek a copy of the letters of administration.

So the death of a sole borrower is a little more complicated and can cause delays in the repayment of the mortgage outstanding. It is common for lenders to suspend the mortgage repayments on the death of a sole borrower until grants of probate or letters of administration are issued and dealt with.

Inheriting a property

If you inherit a property you may be liable to an inheritance tax.

This tax is calculated at a rate of 20% above a threshold amount depending on your relationship with the person from whom you inherited the property.

For example if the beneficiary is a child, including an adopted, fostered or stepchild, the limit to which they can receive a gift or inheritance without having to pay gift tax is €466,725. Any amount above this figure is taxed at 20%.

If the beneficiary is a brother, sister, niece, nephew or ancestor of the person providing the gift or inheritance, the limit is €46,673 and in all other cases it is €22,336.

So if you inherit a property from your uncle valued at €246,673 the first €46,673 is exempt and you will be taxed at 20% of the remaining €200,000 which amounts to €40,000.

The first €3,000 worth of your inheritance is excluded when calaculating your tax bill in any single calendar year.

If the property passed on is the family home no tax will be applicable to the surviving spouse as there is a spouse exemption allowing for any benefit taken either as a gift or inheritance to be exempt from capital acquisitions tax.

There are cases when the inheritance of a home is completely free from inheritance tax provided certain conditions are met:

- The property must have been occupied as their home by the person receiving the inherited property for a minimum of three years prior to the death of the property owner.
- The person inheriting the property must not own or have an interest in another property.
- The beneficiary, if under 55 years old, must continue to own and reside in the property as their family home for a period of at least six years after inheriting the property.
- This inheritance tax exemption will be clawed back though if the person sells the property (if it is not replaced with another) or does not reside in the property for the minimum period of six years after receiving the inheritance.

Converting an endowment-type policy to an interest and capital-type repayment

This is a question that I am frequently asked as many people took out 'endowment' type mortgages in the 1980s and early 1990s. With these types of mortgages, the borrower pays interest to the lender on the full mortgage throughout the term of the mortgage so the original amount borrowed remains the same for the whole mortgage term. The borrower also effects an endowment life-assurance savings policy which is designed to pay off the mortgage should the borrower die before the mortgage is repaid and also to accumulate a cash fund by the end of the policy term which will be sufficient in size to repay the mortgage amount outstanding in full. Therefore the borrower makes two separate repayments – interest to the lender and an endowment premium to the life company.

Repayment of the capital to the lender is deferred until the end of the mortgage term, when it is hoped the endowment policy will mature at a level sufficient to repay the mortgage in full. The popularity of endowment mortgages was mainly due to tax relief availability on the interest paid on the mortgage which did not reduce and also on the policy premiums paid into the life assurance savings policy. Changes in government policy over the years eroded these reliefs: tax relief has not been available on endowment premiums since the early 1990s and the relief on mortgage interest is now given only as a tax credit at standard rate.

The changes in taxation policy together with concerns about the capacity of the policies to repay the mortgage in full at maturity – with the possibility of a capital shortfall instead of a cash surplus as originally envisaged – have reduced the attractiveness of endowment mortgages.

Whether it is a good idea to convert to an interest and capital-type method of repayment will depend on a number of factors. For example, a borrower may wish to convert because they are experiencing financial difficulties and they can reduce their arrears by cashing in their policy. Whatever the reason for surrendering your policy, there are several factors to consider first:

- Life assurance cover attaching to the endowment is lost when you cash it in so you will have to take out a new policy to cover the repayment of your mortgage in the event of your death. How much is this now going to cost you?
- Early surrender of your endowment policy can be pointless as the policy may be worth nothing depending on how long it is in force.
- If you convert to an annuity-type repayment method, your new monthly repayment could be more than what you were previously repaying as you are now paying both interest and capital rather than interest only.
- If you cash in a policy that is 'with profits' this could mean your losing any terminal bonus that may be payable to you when the policy eventually matures.

It is actually up to your mortgage lender whether they allow you to change from an endowment-type repayment to an interest and cap-ital-type repayment. If they do agree to your converting your repayent method you will agree a course of action with them. Normally you will have to have a life policy in place before the endowment policy is cashed in, just in case anything were to happen in the interim, as you do lose life cover when you cash in this type of policy.

When you cash in your endowment policy you get the surrender value credited to your mortgage account. You will have previously agreed a repayment term and product type – for example fixed/variable, tracker or current-account mortgage – with your lender and this will ensure that your loan is repaid in full over the term agreed

The actual process involved in converting to the capital and interest method is pretty straightforward. Firstly the lender and the borrower agree a course of action. The investment policy is surrendered by the customer or with the lender's permission if the policy is assigned. Then the surrender value is credited to the mortgage account and new mortgage repayments are calculated, ensuring that the loan is repaid over the remaining term or over a period negotiated between the two parties.

Credit check yourself

When you apply to a mortgage lender for finance they will do a credit check on you to ensure that you have never been bankrupt or had judgements registered against you, They view your repayment history on current or previous loans.

This is a very important issue with lenders as it allows them to view how you conducted the repayment of previous loans. They can see if you were ever in arrears and if so by how many months. It gives them a graphic picture of your repayment profile.

There are occasions when people apply for a loan and while their ability to pay is without question, they are refused finance because of a poor credit bureau report. It can be very frustrating as you may not remember any loans you had in the past and if you do you may think your repayment record was OK. Of course what you think may be OK and what a lender thinks could be different. A lender will frown upon repeated unpaids or a regular pattern of missed monthly repayments. What a lender views on the bureau record will not tell them why the repayments were missed, just that they were missed.

There can be occasions when you can get bad credit details removed or amended provided the details recorded are incorrect. However, failure to repay a loan on time or failure to keep to the terms of the loan agreement will not be amended on your credit rating. Only the financial institution with which you were dealing has the power to amend your repayment profile.

If you are acting as guarantor for a loan, be very much aware that failure of the person you are helping to meet the repayments on time or failure to repay the loan at all will also reflect on you, The account's profile will duly be recorded under your name as well.

From July 2004 providers of credit cards, for example, have had the option of supplying information on your credit card repayments and can show if cards were ever cancelled or revoked by them. Credit unions have also been invited to join the other members of the scheme, of which there are currently 38.

Any loan details recorded with the bureau will appear for a period of five years from the date the loan was completed.

If you are in any doubt at all about any loans previously held by you which you feel may come against you when applying for any form of credit in the future or which may already have hindered you, you can credit-check yourself and see exactly what every lender will see when you are applying for a loan. A fee of €6 together with a completed request form (available from its website) should be sent to the Irish Credit Bureau, which will in turn forward you its findings.

I cannot stress enough the importance of having a good repayment record as it does have a significant bearing on whether lending institutions will advance funds to you. So whether it is mortgage repayments, car loan repayments – or even how you operate your credit card – make sure you meet the repayments on time. This will, of course, be the result of good planning and careful management of the account from which your monthly commitments are debited.

10
Buying Overseas

Why are we buying abroad?

Over the past number of years the number of Irish people who are purchasing property abroad has increased significantly.

People are typically buying overseas for two main purposes. The first reason is for investment. Disappointed by the current rental market in Ireland, a number of Irish investors are looking overseas for properties they can rent out to earn a reasonable return.

The second reason is for buyers' own personal use, i.e. holidaying. Whilst you may rent out your property and hope that the rental income will repay the mortgage, you will want to take advantage of your property at some time during the year for you and your family's own use. You can probably add your extended family, who will also take advantage of the property – and why not!

So why are we now buying abroad in larger numbers than before? I believe there are a number of contributing factors:

Interest rates

Rates are at an all-time low and are forecast to remain so for the foreseeable future. Money is cheap and being able to borrow funds and repay on an interest-only basis makes purchasing abroad a very attractive and affordable proposition. For example if you borrow €200,000 on an interest-only basis at a rate of 3.5% your monthly repayment will be just €583.

Prices overseas

The location you are considering buying in coupled with demand for and supply of property in that area will have a direct influence on the price of property. This applies not only to purchasing in Ireland but to purchasing overseas.

Countries that joined the EU in 2004 – Cyprus, Czech Republic, Estonia, Latvia, Lithuania, Hungary, Malta, Poland, Slovenia and Slovakia – have attracted much attention from Irish investors since their accession, obviously some more so than others. They are attractive for a number of reasons, – beautiful cities; beautiful countryside; breathtaking scenery; their weather; and their cost of living – but the biggest influence has to be how cheap it is to buy property in these countries, as well as many others.

A property in the likes of Prague, Budapest or Warsaw, for example, can be bought for as little as €80,000–€90,000, compared to purchasing a one-bed apartment in Portugal or parts of Spain or France that will cost more than €200,000. So people who cannot afford a property in excess of €200,000 will look at purchasing in countries with lower entry levels.

Property values increasing at home

Property values in Ireland have increased significantly over the past 10 years. In some areas of Dublin, for example, property has increased by 300% since 1995. So as our mortgages have been reducing and the value of our properties increasing, the amount of equity we find in our homes has increased significantly.

If you purchased a property for €100,000 in 1995 and borrowed €90,000 the equity you had in your property back then was €10,000. Fast forward 10 years. Your property is now worth €300,000 and the mortgage outstanding now is €65,000. You therefore have equity in your property worth €235,000.

By remortgaging or releasing this equity we can now finance the purchase of other properties in a very easy and affordable way.

Considerations to be borne in mind when purchasing a property abroad

- Find out first and foremost how much you can afford to borrow from both your Irish and overseas lender. Find out what other costs you are likely to incur as well as the purchase price, for example set-up costs, onging expenses, legal fees and taxes. These additional costs can set you back more than 10% of the cost of the property.

- Research all legal issues and costs involved. Find a solicitor who has experience with overseas purchase and who can advise and assist you. Before you buy anywhere it is extremely important to be fully aware of the legal process and additional costs associated with your purchase and the potential tax implications of buying abroad. Never sign a contract you do not understand.

- How much is the property going to cost you each year aside from your mortgage repayments? It's all well and good factoring in rental income when deciding where and when to buy but your annual outgoings must be considered. Are you going to manage the property yourself or are you going to employ a managing agent to oversee everything from renting it to having it cleaned and kept in good repair.

- If you are buying a property purely for investment reasons what is your annual return going to be? This is normally calculated as the annual rental income expressed as a percentage of the purchase price of the property. So if a property cost you €150,000 and your rental income is €6,000 your annual yield or return is 4%. You must also consider what your net return is after you deduct all overheads from your annual rental income. Anything between 4% and 6% is considered a reasonable return.

- To achieve reasonable returns on your property expect to rent your property for at least 30 weeks in any one year.

- Research the area in which you are purchasing. Those who have made successful property purchases for investment in the past have done their homework on the areas in which they bought. It is hard to do the necessary research on a weekend visit to an area. You need to spend more time in the area to get a feel for it, view other developments and compare prices and value for money and ask the locals for their assistance with some of your questions. This may be easier said than done as time and affordability may mean that frequent visits are not realistic for you but if you can visit more often you may reap the rewards in the long run.

- If you are arranging finance to purchase a property ensure a clause is inserted in the contract to say 'subject to mortgage approval' just in case you cannot get a loan. This may ensure that any deposit paid is refundable.

- Ensure that you do not inherit any debt on the property. Get your solicitor to double-check this. For example the developer you are purchasing from could have borrowed moneys to build your development and the amount borrowed may have been allocated against each plot as additional security for the developer's bank.

- Get a structural valuation carried out on the property if it is second-hand.

- Buy in a country that is easily accessible by plane and preferably sunny.

- Try to buy a property with at least two bedrooms, as this will make the property more desirable to the rental market.

- Buy in a location that is reasonably close to an airport – not more than a 45- minute drive – and within easy distance of local amenities, golf courses or beaches.

Financing your purchase
Option 1

The majority of Irish lending institutions will not advance funds to purchase a property overseas. They will, however, advance money to you on an Irish-based property on which they can obtain a legal charge. A lender in Ireland is not interested in the property you are purchasing abroad; they are interested in the property you are using in Ireland to raise the money that will be used to fund your purchase overseas.

Many people now have very valuable properties with small mortgages outstanding on them so they are considering releasing sufficient equity from their property to allow them to purchase overseas. With interest rates so low, the possibility of doing this on an interst-only basis makes repayments very affordable.

An Irish lending institution will therefore be prepared to advance funds to you once they are satisfied with the security you are offering them and your ability to repay the amount required on the basis of your earned income – excluding foreign rental income. Finally they will want confirmation that the funds you are raising are actually going towards a the purchase of a property abroad.

There are, however, some lenders here in Ireland with specialist overseas lending teams that are prepared to advance funds to you if you are purchasing in, for example, the UK. They will use the property in the UK as security on its own. The amount they will advance will depend on the strength of the borrower but typically it will not exceed 85% of the purchase price of the property.

Your first option to finance the purchase of a property abroad is to raise 100% of the purchase price from an Irish-based property owned by you. A lender will be prepared to advance the amount provided they can get a legal charge over the property, if they are satisfied with your ability to repay, and if the amount advanced does not exceed 85% of the value of the property, including taking over any existing debt secured on the property.

A lending institution will usually require the following from you if you are prepared to proceed with this option:

- Their interest will have to be noted in a fire policy covering the property.
- A statement of affairs may have to be provided to the lender.
- Evidence of adequate surplus income showing an ability to repay the amount required excluding potential foreign rental income.
- Valuation carried out on the property confirming its current market value.
- Life cover may be requested.

Some common features pertaining to such a loan will include:

Interest rates

The security given – whether the property is your principal private residence or an investment property you are using to raise funds against will determine the rate on offer:

- Private residences will attract standard home-loan rates whilst investment properties could be 0.5% above home-loan rates.
- Fixed-rate options would be available.
- Interest-only facilities for up to ten years or for the whole term of the mortgage could be made available if required but this will depend on the lending institution.

Term

Typically up to 25 years or longer, provided the loan is repaid in full by the time the borrower reaches the age of 65 or 70, depending on the lender).

Arrangement fee

None

Legal/valuation fees

Paid by the borrower (depending on the lending institution, which may make a contribution towards legal fees)

Option 2

The second option available to those looking to purchase a property overseas is to raise a mortgage from a bank in the country where you are purchasing.

The amount a bank will advance will vary from country to country, as will the percentage of the purchase price they are prepared to advance, the maximum term they are willing to offer, the minimum amount they will advance and the interest rates they will offer. Mortgage lenders across Europe will assess your ability to borrow based upon your net income: your total outgoings both at home and with your new loan should not exceed a maximum of 40% of your monthly net income.

Below is a guide to the eligibility in some popular countries in which Irish people currently buy property:

Spain
- Minimum loan amount of €50,000 available to a maximum of 85% of the value of the property.
- Maximum term is 30 years.
- Interest-only options are available but this will depend on the lender and the amount you are borrowing. Some will offer you this option only if you are borrowing less than 60% of the purchase price of the property.
- Fixed and variable-rate options available.

England
- Minimum loan amount of £50,000 available to a maximum of 85% of the value of the property.
- Maximum term is 25 years.
- Interest-only options available depending on how much you are borrowing against the value of the property.
- Arrangement fees can range from 0.5% to 1% of the loan amount but can be waived depending on the strength of the case.
- Fixed rates and variable-rates options are available.
- Rates ranging from 6.25% in sterling.

France
- Minimum loan amount is €70,000 available to a maximum of 85% of the value of the property.
- Maximum term is 25 years.
- Interest-only options are available but will depend on the lender and the amount you are borrowing.
- Fixed and variable-rate options available.

Florida
- Minimum loan amount is $100,000 available to a maximum of 80% of the value of the property.
- Maximum term is 30 years, borrowing in US dollars.

- Mortgage lenders in Florida determine the loan available after a credit search and point-scoring system.
- Fixed and variable-rate options available in US dollars.

Poland

- Minimum loan amount is €50,000 available to a maximum of 70% of the value of the property.
- Maximum term is 20 years.
- Interest-only options are not available.
- You can borrow in US dollars or euro.

The minimum loan amounts and maximum percentages offered by banks in each of the above countries will change quite often to meet demand and you may find that you can borrow a higher (or be limited to a lower) amount than outlined above; such is the fast pace at which banks have to respond to an ever-changing market.

You will still have to make up the shortfall between what you are receiving from your foreign lender and the purchase price of the property. So how do you make up the difference?

You do it exactly the same way as outlined in option 1 but rather than securing 100% of the purchase price by releasing equity on your Irish-based property you release just 20%, 30% or whatever is required, depending on how much your foreign bank is prepared to lend to you.

For example, if the purchase price of your property abroad is €200,000 and you have secured an 80% mortgage on it, i.e. €160,000, you will need €40,000 to complete the purchase (excluding legal fees, taxes etc.). You have a property here in Ireland valued at €400,000 and you have a mortgage of €100,000 outstanding on it. So you will need to release €40,000 from your Irish property and will do so by either (a) your current lender releasing this sum by way of an equity-release type loan or (b) remortgaging your existing loan and moving it to another lender, including the extra €40,000 when doing so.

Option 3

What happens if you secure an 80% facility from a foreign lender but you either (a) do not have the 20% required in savings or (b) you do not have a property with enough equity in it to release the 20% needed or (c) you are not prepared to raise funds from an Irish-based property even if there is sufficient equity in the property. A solution may be to secure a personal loan from an Irish lender to fund the difference.

However, it is worth noting what a lender will require in order to consider sanctioning such a loan:

Security
Assigned life policy for the amount and term of the loan

Rate
A margin of up to 2.5% above the lender's home-loan rate would not be unexpected.

Term
Maximum 15-year period

Arrangement fee
1% of the loan amount

Legal fees
If applicable, paid by the borrower

Profile of borrower
A statement of net worth: lenders may insist that this should show that the borrower has a net worth of at least €2 million, excluding the family home's market value

Lenders will require evidence of your ability to repay the amount requested along with all other outstanding debt.

11
Financial Review

Review your finances

There is never a good or a bad time to start reviewing your personal finances. It should be done now so as to ensure that what you currently have put in place is sufficient for you and your family. Areas that should be addressed are:

- Do you have an additional life-assurance requirement?
- What are your current pension provisions and will they be sufficient in retirement?
- What would happen if you were to suffer a serious illness?
- Do you have a savings plan in place?
- Is your income sufficiently covered in the event of your being unable to work should you suffer an accident or illness?
- Have you made a will?

These are issues that we tend not to address straight away. We promise ourselves that we will do it at some stage in the future. It may be that we do not know where to start or whom to ask for advice but we also know that it must be done and that, yes, we do need to review, for example, the level of independent life cover we have. Is it sufficient in the event of our death? Not a nice question to address but a very important one to consider.

If you were to pass away, would you like your dependants to continue to enjoy their current standard of living or to suffer a significant drop in their quality of life? Of course you would not want this to happen, so what are you going to do about it? Nothing for the moment? Or are you going to put cover in place immediately and rest easy, knowing that your loved ones would be looked after.

I am specifically referring to independent life cover, and sometimes the amount of cover taken out by people is surprising What is the right amount? Four times your income? Five times? Is €200,000 too little, €500,000 too much? The answer is that the level of life cover required should be sufficient to replace your net monthly income.

You have to consider, for example, monthly income payable on your death such as a pension paid to your spouse from your employer, the widow's state pension, investment income if any. You also have to deduct the amount of money that you would have spent on yourself on a monthly basis. There will be no more mortgage repayments (assuming your mortgage is protected by a life policy), insurance payments or death in service payments. Having considered all the above you can arrive at a figure that is sufficient to replace your income, but the most important thing, I believe, is understanding why you need that particular level of cover. You will know then that you are neither over- nor underinsured.

Below is an example of what I mean by factoring in the losses and gains of income in death so you arrive at the correct level of cover.

This individual has a net monthly income of   €2,820:
Life insurance summary:
If a fatal accident were to happen, his family would:
need to cover his monthly income of   €2,820

Less: Monthly income payable on his death:
Employer's pension   €0
Widow's state pension approximately
(two dependent children)   €930
Investment income (rental income, share, dividends etc)   €0

Less: Monthly income no longer required:
Amount on self   €400
Mortgage repayment (covered by mortgage protection)   €970
Insurance repayments   €120
Monthly income required/shortfall   **€400**

To compensate fully for this change would require a lump sum of €192,000 less
His existing level of life cover   €32,000
Death in service benefit if any   €0
Liquid assets – cashed within 6 months   €0
This means that he would need
additional life cover of   €160,000
Both lump sums when invested at a net rate of 2.5% would generate an income
of €400 per month whilst maintaining the initial capital sum

You also have to look at replacing your income in the event of your being unable to work for a period of time due to an accident or illness.

Let me tell you about a client of mine of whose income was €2,600 per month. His wife did not work. His employer would pay his salary in full for two months in the event of his being unable to work due to an accident or illness. Whilst this is a reasonable length of time to have cover from his employer, his being out of work for longer than eight weeks would have a very serious effect on his income and quality of life. Let me tell you why!

His only income after this eight-week period would be a disability benefit of approximately €293 per week. This means that he would have an income shortfall of €1,400 per month! Bearing in mind that his mortgage would have to be paid, as well as bills and food, there would obviously be insufficient income available each month to meet these demands.

This startled him a great deal and he immediately went about protecting his income in case he should suffer an illness that would keep him from working and earning an income. The other startling thing was that it cost him only €22 per month to put cover in place that would pay 75% of his salary if he was out of work due to an illness.

Of course to put all these things into place comes at a monthly cost. What has to be considered is affordability, and you need to prioritise what is most important to you right now and put that in place immediately. For instance, you may wish to increase your life cover initially because you have young children; you may wish to put income replacement into force straight away because you are self-employed; you may wish to address your income in retirement now as you have only twenty years to retirement – and so on.

I have outlined below a sample cashflow statement of a family, showing their income and outgoings each month. This shows the amoung of surplus cash left over each month that can be used towards putting in place a specific product, for example extra life assurance, income replacement, pension, or whatever is most important to them at the present time.

Cashflow Summary
Income from employment

Mr. A. Another – XYZ Limited	€2,800
Mrs. B. Another – ABC Limited	€1,800
Other sources of income	
Interest from Irish Banks & Building Societies	€0
Dividends from companies	€0
Total income:	€4,600
Less:	

Fixed expenses

Mortgage	
ABC Lending institution – Number 060170	€600
ABC Lending institution – Number 300501	€200
Loan Repayments	
EFG Leasing company – Number 120670	€200
Life Insurance	
A Life Company – Policy number 060204	€50
Regular Savings	
SSIA Account number 140789	€100
Property Insurance	
A Insurance Company – Ref: 260643	€40
Dependants' Care	€0

Other Expenses

Home expenses	€600
Bills	€400
Food	€800
Supporting others	€0
Sports & Leisure	€50
School/Cars/Transport	€300
Healthcare expenses (VHI/BUPA)	€100
Childcare	€800
Total Outgoings:	€4,240-
Total Monthly Cashflow	€360+

By reviewing your financial position you will get an overview of what you should have or what you have too much of. What you want is to strike a balance and address any issues which are of particular importance to you and your family. If you carry out such a financial review what you will have is a plan in place which will give you tremendous focus on what needs to be done and – when this plan is implemented – great peace of mind.

Glossary of Mortgage Terms

APR
The annual percentage rate. It is defined in the Consumer Credit Act (1995) with the intention of providing a basis for comparing different forms of credit. It takes into account most of the up-front and ongoing costs involved when taking out a mortgage.

Arrangement fee
A fee paid to the lender in return for providing you with a mortgage. It is usually paid on completion and applies only to certain commercial mortgages or when arranging finance to purchase overseas.

Assignment
A document transferring the rights of ownership from one person to another. An example of this is when you assign a life policy to your lender as conditioned in your mortgage-offer letter.

Auction
A public sale of a property to the highest bidder. The successful purchaser must sign a binding contract immediately so they should ensure that all valuations and mortgage approval are in place prior to the auction.

Buildings' insurance
This covers the cost of rebuilding the structure of the property if it is damaged. All lenders will insist that they have their interest noted in the policy.

Bridging loan

A short-term loan facility to allow you purchase your new property prior to the completed sale of your existing property. You may wish to complete the purchase of your new property before you receive the proceeds of the sale of your existing property so this temporary loan will allow you to complete the purchase. When the sale of your property does complete you will then redeem this bridging facility. Before a lender will grant this facility they will want confirmation that unconditional contracts have been signed for the sale of your existing property.

Buy to let

A property purchased to rent out to others.

Capital and interest

The two parts of which your monthly mortgage repayment is made up. One part will go towards servicing the interest on the amount you borrowed and the other will be used to repay the amount outstanding.

Contracts

A written legal agreement by which the purchaser and owner of a property agree to buy and sell the property.

Conveyancing

The legal process involved in buying and selling a property.

Credit search

A check your lender will make with the Irish Credit Bureau to find out whether you have any judgements registered against you and what your repayment record has been like on loans you currently have or loans you have had with other lending institutions.

Deposit

The amount of money you put down towards the purchase of a property.

Discounted rate
An interest rate which is set at a margin below a lender's standard variable rate. This reduction will last for an agreed period of time, usually six, twelve or 24 months, depending on your lender.

Equity
The amount of value in your property that is not covered by your mortgage. Take the amount of your mortgage from the value of the property to work out your equity.

Easement
A right of way which the owner of one property has over an adjoining property.

Endowment
A savings/investment policy which is designed to produce a lump sum to pay off an interest-only type mortgage.

Fixed rate
The interest rate charged to your mortgage which is set for an agreed period.

Freehold
This is where you own the property and the land it stands on.

Gazumping
When a person selling a property accepts an offer from a buyer but then accepts a higher offer from another buyer before contracts are signed.

Guarantor
This is a person who agrees to guarantee a loan. They are liable for the repayment if the borrower fails to maintain the mortgage repayments. A guarantor is usually a parent or close family relative.

HomeBond
This is a ten-year guarantee against major structural defects in your property. It also provides against water and smoke damage for the

first two years. Finally, it will cover you against the loss of stage payments before a new house is completed should the builder declare bankruptcy or go into liquidation.

HB47

This is a certificate issued by HomeBond confirming that the property purchased is covered under the HomeBond guarantee scheme.

Indemnity bond

This is a once-off fee paid by the borrower to the lender if the amount advanced is more than a certain percentage of the property's value. It is designed to protect the lender and help them to recover the total amount outstanding should you default on the loan and if they cannot realise the full amount owing to them from the sale of the repossessed property. It offers no protection to the borrower and is a very costly additional expense. Many lenders have now decided not to charge this fee to homeowners and instead absorb the cost themselves.

Interest-only mortgage

A mortgage in which the borrower is required to pay interest only on the amount borrowed to the lender for a specific term. Interest-only repayments can range from three years to the full mortgage term. It is the borrower's responsibility to ensure that sufficient funds exist to repay the mortgage in full at the end of the mortgage term.

Leasehold

An arrangement by which you own the property for a set number of years but not the land it stands on.

LTV

Loan to value. This is the size of your mortgage as a percentage of the property's value. If your mortgage is €200,000 and the property is valued at €400,00 the loan to value is 50% i.e. €200,000/€400,000.

Life assurance
An insurance policy that pays out a lump sum on the death of a borrower which will then be used to repay the mortgage amount outstanding.

Mortgagee
The lending agency that lends you the money to purchase your property.

Mortgager
The person taking out the mortgage.

Mortgage repayment protection
An insurance policy that covers against accident, illness or redundancy. It provides a monthly payment towards your mortgage repayments if you are unable to work for an extended period due to any of these circumstances. The cost of this cover is about €5 for every €100 of your mortgage repayment you wish to have covered.

Negative equity
Where the money you owe on the mortgage is greater than the value of the property.

Premier guarantee
This is very similar to HomeBond. It includes a structural guarantee for ten years as well as water- and smoke-damage protection, and guards against the builder going bankrupt.

Pension mortgage
An interest-only type of mortgage combined with a personal or occupational-type pension plan. On retirement the borrower is expected to repay the mortgage outstanding from the lump sum benefit available under the pension agreement. The main attractions of a pension mortgage are the tax benefits available in funding a pension.

Remortgage

The process of paying off one mortgage with the proceeds from a new mortgage, using the same property as security.

Redemption penalty

A penalty charged by a lender when a borrower pays off their mortgage before the end of an agreed fixed-rate period.

Searches

Checks carried out by your solicitor to ensure that, for example, the person selling the property is entitled to sell the property; that they have no judgements registered against them; and that the builder you are buying from has not gone bankrupt.

Snag list

This is arranged by the purchaser of a new home to ensure that any defects in their property that need to be fixed are completed before they hand over the final moneys.

Stamp duty

A government tax on the purchase of a property. The value of the property you are purchasing and your status – such as whether you are a first-time buyer or investor – will determine the amount of stamp duty that is payable.

Shared ownership

A scheme operated by a housing authority where a person owns part of the property and pays a mortgage on this part while the housing authority owns the rest of the property and the person pays rent on this.

Structural survey

A comprehensive report carried out on the inside and outside of the property you are purchasing by a qualified architect/engineer.

Term

The period of years over which you have taken out the mortgage.

Title deeds
Documents that show who owns the property.

Transfer deed
The document signed by both the seller and buyer, transferring the ownership of the property from one to the other.

Unencumbered
This is where the property is owned outright with no mortgages or loans secured against it.

Valuation
A survey carried out by the lender to find out how much a property is worth and whether it is suitable to lend a mortgage on.

Variable rate
An interest rate a lender charges that can go up or down, with your monthly repayments changing accordingly.

Vendor
The person selling the property.

Finally, remember that your home may be repossessed if you do not keep up repayments on your mortgage. You are advised to think carefully before securing any other debt against your home.